ADVANCE
THE OVERTHINKE

"Through her own curious, brave, and compelling quest for love and self-knowledge, Kristen invites you to question everything and to make your life your experiment. There is wisdom here."

–Dr. Duana Welch, Ph.D.

Social Scientist & Author of *Love Factually: 10 Proven Steps from I Wish to I Do*

"A deeply moving, heartwarming collection of uncensored, poignant and often quite funny tales from a millennial woman's dedicated explorations of herself and ideas about relationship, intimacy and love. The additional bonus: Kristen offers up simple, thoughtful exercises [and] experiments to support other intrepid seekers exploring this evermore complex terrain."

–Robyn L. Posin, Ph.D.

Psychologist & Author of *Choosing Gentleness: Opening Our Hearts to All the Ways We Feel & Are in Every Moment*

"Love is not a script we learn. It's a way of being on a road to deeper freedom. With wit, curiosity, and well-earned wisdom, Kristen Smith helps you chart your own course to the love that's true for you. If you let it, this book can change your life."

–Edwina Barvosa, Ph.D.

Social Scientist & Professor, UC Santa Barbara

"It is a rare dual talent that can honor both left brain and right brain. This lucid and compelling exploration of a love and intimacy beyond the anemic cultural narrative of "normal" regarding who and how we should love, clears shame and inspires authenticity with a beguiling blend of wry humor, intellect, and heartwarming honesty."

–Kim Bryson, RScP

Certified Clinical Sexologist, Sex Educator and Coach

THE OVERTHINKER'S GUIDE TO LOVE

a story of real-life experiments
turned practical wisdom

KRISTEN RUTH SMITH

For everyone who's ever been
told they're doing it wrong.

CONTENTS

INTRODUCTION

Hello, my fellow overthinker! You analyzer, ponder-er, planner, and over-complicate-er. I am so happy to be in the presence of such a like-minded investigator of life. I realize that in these strange and surprising times, our ranks are growing rapidly, and if you are new to overthinking you may still be uncertain of whether you've firmly earned the designation. So, let's put your mind at ease with a few quick questions, shall we?

Quiz: Are You an Overthinker?

1. You are interested in the deeper *why* of everything going on around you.

2. You have a running one, five, and ten-year plan as well as B and C variants of each.

3. You take your time before acting; your thinking to doing ratio hovers around 5:1.

4. Change doesn't bother you … so long as you have fair warning and are given sufficient time to incorporate said change into your pre-existing master plan.

5. You have, at various times, been categorized by those around you as dependable, a perfectionist, and an inflexible pain in the butt.

6. You order a meal like you're in a scene of *When Harry Met Sally*.

7. Lists turn you on.

8. You have a mind like a steel trap, remembering verbatim what someone said even when they don't remember themselves.

9. You are good at picking up social cues in new situations because you're such a keen observer, but you often feel low grade suspicion that you're missing something everyone else in the room already knows.

10. You replay conversations in your head—good or bad—and run them through a football-game-post-show style analysis.

11. You love the white knight feeling that arises when someone spontaneously needs something (gum, aspirin, a safety pin), the more unusual the better (an obscure 90s pop culture reference, a kidney), and you just happen to have one on you.

12. You mull over the events of your life until you're able to find meaning in everything.

So, how'd you do? Did you answer yes to three? Eight? All twelve? Sounds like you're in the right place! We overthinkers live in our heads. We have strong voices in there, sensible voices, voices that ensure we're making the best decisions for our families, the most logical choices for our careers, keeping us safe in matters of personal risk and preventing potential disasters. We keep our options open while at the same time laying out dependable long-term contingency plans. We prepare. We can effortlessly see the steps necessary to get us from point A to point B. We're good friends to calendars and spreadsheets. When someone needs to know a birthdate or someone's food allergies, we can provide that information instantaneously and unequivocally.

And that makes us awesome! Our skill sets make us the people who get sh★t done, who translate someone's vague ideas into actionable steps. We are expert chaos wranglers. We are the ones who make the world work in an orderly fashion so that everyone else can live in it.

Because we are observers. We watch people. We track crowds and cultures. We recognize patterns. We take in an incredible amount of information and digest it, assimilate it, and hold it until it can be of use. We are constantly trying to figure things out. Our brains hunger for orderly understanding. We crave clarity. We relax in the presence of direct, digestible logic. We sort. We anticipate. We plan. We are born to approach society with the eye of a scientist or anthropologist. And *this* is why I've sought you out, my fellow overthinker. The Love Lab can always use a new scientist.

Welcome to the Love Lab

Yes, the Love Lab. Welcome! Never has this inquiry been more needed. In a landscape of rapidly changing ever-more-fluid understandings of sexuality, partnership, mating and romance, more and more of us have become overthinkers when it comes to love. This field is the final frontier right now. Sexual and gender definitions in particular have jumped leaps and bounds in just a few years, and I want to be among the pioneers who ride the edge of the wave. I want to see whether it's possible for us to get so specific in defining each individual experience of love that we might, in the end, consider un-definition the norm.

I'll admit that it's a bit of a personal mission. You see, I've lived my entire life without a clear internal sexual compass, so even though I, like most of us, grew up with pretty straightforward instructions of how I was supposed to engage with love and romance, I still found the entire endeavor to be baffling. None of the forever-partnerships being modeled looked appealing to me, neither the more traditional faire of my Midwestern family nor the more alternative samplings that were just beginning to surge in the media and larger world around me. I didn't see myself in any of it. I didn't know how to do romantic relationship, and I got the message that the intimacy I brought to my non-romantic relationships was 'unusual.' I knew I was doing it wrong.

Then, the rules seemed to get blown up. Gone were the days of assumptions, of 'supposed to,' of culturally scripted love and marriage plays. Yet, in this sea of options, I felt somehow even more a failure at love. I was nearly thirty and still couldn't wrap my head around romantic relationship, let alone sex, because I still had no idea how to define myself. How could I explain my intentions to a potential partner when I couldn't even parse for myself where my desires fell within the newly expanded lexicon of sexual self-definitions? And how could I figure that out without gaining relational experience with a partner? It was a classic Catch 22.

I began to wonder how many others might also be excited at the sheer number of possibilities for their future relationships, but also completely overwhelmed as to how to navigate this newly expanded love buffet. Thus became the mission of the Love Lab. Yes, we all have the option to define our experience of love however we like these days, but can we make room on that stage for the un-defined as well? Can we, in fact, invite the questioning and investigation? Can we return Love to her natural state of a miracle to be discovered? I have to believe we can, and I certainly want to try!

Every good discovery begins with genuine curiosity and a healthy dose of, "I don't know." This is a safe place to not know. In this work we each begin with what we think we know, and then make a conscious effort to unknow it. We stop defining love so that we might discover it. We seek to explore and express who we might be in love in a given moment, and when fresh incoming data changes the trajectory of an experiment, we excitedly explore each new hypothesis without bias.

We who choose a life in the Love Lab are both its scientists and subjects. Each field scientist is collecting experiences, data, and making observations out in the wild that help all of us further fill in the puzzle of what it means for a human being to be in love. We approach love as a succession of small experiments, each one building upon the next, each one informing the direction of the next inquiry. We share incoming data, experiences, points of view, and theories with one another. We collaborate. And we hope to better understand the vast scope of what love can look like.

So, please feel free to leave your self-definitions and pre-conceived notions at the door. In fact, I must insist that you do. It's standard clean room procedure that we not bring any outside contaminants into the lab. These are delicate and often unpredictable experiments we're running in here, so we must do our best to protect them from the taint of what we think we've already defined. Fear not, you'll be allowed to pick your definitions up on your way out if you so choose; though I'll be honest, more often than not newcomers find that these items no longer fit quite as well upon departure.

Have I mentioned how excited I am that you've chosen this particular day to join us? I mentioned that one of the most crucial parts of the Love Lab is the opportunity to collaborate with other highly skilled overthinkers, to pool data in hopes of gaining a larger view and recognizing any possible Universal Love Laws. Well, it just so happens that today is my turn to share my findings!

The Debriefing

I have been deployed in the field for over three decades now. I was deep in the weeds, uncertain where I was heading with only the vaguest sense that I was even going the correct direction. At times it was hard to see more than a few feet in front of my face. The map I cobbled together out there was hand drawn and covered in scribbles and cryptic notes of 'here lie monsters,' but it was the best I had to work with. So unless I wanted to stand in the weeds forever, I had to take my next step, perform the next experiment, collect the next specimen, observe the next small sliver of data, and hope the new information would shine some light on my course. I've returned now, happily reunited with my fellow collogues, with a rucksack full of smudged field journals.

What follows is a record of my experiences out there. Each of the sixteen experimental reports I present to you here is prefaced by the working hypothesis I held going into it and the methods I employed. At the end of each, I offer you my data analysis, the learnings I gleaned, as well as the Universal Love Laws suggested in the form of a conclusion.

You will also note that at the end of each report I have offered an experiment for you to run yourself in hopes that I might more fully communicate my new understanding and that we might collaborate and compare results. I look forward to your insights and hope you'll share them with me at the end of all of this though the lab portal.

But, of course, there's time for that later. For now, let us begin the debriefing.

PART I

Working Hypothesis

CHAPTER ONE

Life is Our Love Laboratory

lab·o·ra·to·ry /ˈlabrəˌtôrē/:
a place equipped to conduct scientific experiments, research, tests, investigations, or analysis; or provide opportunity for experimentation, observation, and practice.

SUBJECT: Overthinker; Female; Age 30 years, 2 months, 28 days.

HYPOTHESIS: I have never spoken about sex or dating around my parents in order to keep them from being able to form any ideas or opinions about my romantic identity. This blank slate state will be maintained until I choose to inform them of my thoughts on the subject.

METHOD: Sibling re-con, a cocktail feint, an escape vehicle.

FIELD SITE: A strategically orchestrated Fourth of July gathering at my home on the family orchard.

Experiment 140.07.3:

"You know, Mom is convinced you're coming out to them."

"What!?"

"She kept asking me why you wanted everyone to come down for the Fourth. I told her you just wanted to see us for the holiday, but she knows something's up. Now she's telling me that I *have* to tell her if you're going to tell them you're gay. So she can prepare herself."

I was taken aback. The suggestion that my parents come visit me in California at the family orchard for the fourth of July weekend wasn't so strange a request. With my granddad's passing a month ago, they'd been planning a return anyway to deal with his affairs. I'd known, of course, when I asked my younger sister to come down it would send up red flags for her, but I didn't really have much of a choice there. I needed the emotional back up. She and I had had a rough relationship growing up, but as is often the case, as adults we'd become allies verging on friends. I was relieved she'd be sitting beside me this evening.

I was almost amused by this report of my mother's frankness. Certainly, I'd known that there was an unspoken wondering around my lack of boyfriends, lifelong virginity, and general disinterest in dating, but to hear that Mom had so boldly verbalized what I took to be one of her biggest fears was a new development. "I can't believe she actually said that to you."

"I know, right? So, how are you doing?"

I shrugged in response. "I'm okay. Ready to just get the whole thing over with. They think we're going to dinner, so if you can suggest cocktails around six, I'll do it then. I figure you and I should actually go out as soon as it's done to let them process."

"How do you think they're going to react?"

"Honestly, I have no idea." I looked to her, "Do you? I mean, I keep trying to get my mind to conjure up some sort of possible outcome here, but it's just blank. It's like this is so outside of the realm of any conversation I ever thought I'd be having with them that even my imagination has thrown up its hands and said, *Don't ask me!*"

My sister's gaze rolled upward as if consulting her own imagination, "Nope, you're right. There's no point of reference for this one."

I hid for most of the day. That wasn't hard on thirty acres of orange trees. Living on a working orchard meant I could always reliably find dust and cobwebs that needed addressing. While I scrubbed my tiny apartment cottage my parents milled around what had been my grandparents' home only a hundred yards away. It was larger and more comfortable, but like mine, it was still a hand-built ranch house, which meant any right angle in the place was only right-ish, and the electrical and plumbing systems had been McGyver-ed in some fashion over the years. I'd come to this orchard from Chicago every year since I'd been born, so moving in four years earlier had felt a little like coming home. At the time I hadn't thought I'd be staying long, but now as I stood at my sink thoroughly washing a dish for the second time, I found myself quietly wondering whether I would move into my grandparents' now vacant house with its dishwasher and laundry room. In the face of my granddad's passing, some part of me was planning to be here for a while.

Despite my self-distraction methods, the hours ticking down to six o'clock were excruciating. With each minute the freight train of my reality barreled forward on its collision course with that in which my parents resided. I anxiously anticipated the moment of impact while my mother and father sat sipping tea in the metaphoric dining car, blissfully unaware of our merging tracks. Finally, it was time. I walked up to the house and let myself in. I could hear the hairdryer whirring in my mother's bathroom. My father emerged from their room still looping his belt. I could only look my sister in the eyes. For once she was ahead of schedule, already dressed, her makeup and hair done, waiting for me.

She made the loud suggestion that we all have a pre-dinner drink on the patio as planned. I was jittery as she herded both of them out the door. My mother finished telling some story as she wandered toward a rattan chair. My father distracted, wrapping up something on his phone. Neither had noticed I'd joined them without a drink in hand. They hovered in front of their seats, but I couldn't hold back any longer. The dam broke. The words rushed out of me awkwardly, "Well, I don't know what your plans are for January, but you're both going to be grandparents."

Seriously, that's how I said it. For all of my overthinker's tendencies, I hadn't been able to envision this moment let alone plan for it.

My father seamlessly stood back up without ever changing his facial expression nor looking towards me. He walked a few steps toward the tree line of the orchard where a large pile of cardboard boxes sat waiting to be broken down. In black leather driving shoes and pressed slacks, he began to slowly and methodically rip them into flat sheets one-by-one. -*Riiiip*- My mother's gaze shifted to my younger sister sitting beside me—my married sister who had always planned on having children—expectantly. She didn't say anything, but made a deferring gesture in my direction. My mother's eyes followed the indication of her fingers to my lap, up to my face, and looped back to my sister. Again, expectantly. Again, my sister remained silent.

In the lightening crack of understanding that passed through her, I released a breath and felt the impact of our realities slamming into one another and merging. Okay, we were all riding the same train again.

"Who's the father?"

"Jonah."

"Does he know?"

"I told him yesterday."

My answer was punctuated by the sound of my father's progress on the cardboard deconstruction project: -*Riiiip*-

"Is he going to be involved?"

"It looks like it."

-*Riiiiiiiiiiiiiip*-

"Are you dating?"

-*Riiiiiiiiiiiiiip*-

"No, we were never together. We don't want to be. We're friends."

"How far are you?"

"Three months. I'm through the first trimester. I'm due the second week of January."

My mother looked at me as though she was meeting me for the first time, her hands in her lap, considering, digesting. Or maybe just slipping into shock. "I'm almost relieved it's someone we know."

-*Riiiiiiip*-

"And we know he's a good guy. And educated. And he's good looking." Her eyes welled.

-*Riiiip*-

"If you want to," I ventured, "I have an ultrasound—"

She quickly waved me off as I went to reach for the grainy black and white photo I'd tucked into the book on the coffee table with a sharp, "No, no. I can't. Not yet." I retracted my hand, a little stung, and returned to answering only the questions that were asked of me. I knew I had to give them time. I had to let them set the pace.

"Have you told any of our family yet? On facebook or anything?"

"No."

"Okay. Don't, okay? I just want to deal with telling Aunt Betty. And Sarah. And Cousin Carol." My mother's face spoke dread, already suffering the imagined chastisements of the more conservative relatives. And the church. And the whole of the Midwest. Not so much their chastisement of me, I presumed, as her failures as a mother.

I told her gently, "I'm okay with you being the one to tell the family if you want to."

She nodded. My mother continued to ask questions in fits and starts, tears and disbelief both playing large roles. As topics turned more toward the logistics of pregnancy, however, I noticed a shift. She became a mother speaking to a mother-to-be rather than to a baffling daughter. My father did eventually rejoin us, though he remained more or less a silent participant.

"Well," I took advantage of a lull in conversation, "Kiki and I were thinking that we would go to dinner and leave you two to have some time alone." I knew there was going to be a lot to process between the two of them that night, and for my own sake, I wanted to be out of earshot of their grief. When my sister and I were safely in the car, I slid the keys into the ignition and turned to her. "Well, that went just about as well as I could have hoped!"

"Yeah!" Her head bobbed in agreement, "Plus, now when you *do* come out to them, instead of being upset they'll just be relieved you're not pregnant again."

Data Analysis:

Love may be a simple word for some, but for an overthinker it can be an elusive concept, and as culture shifts and options abound, more and more of us are overthinking it. The concept of a fixed, comprehendible romantic identity has begun to feel puzzling to many of us. I've been eternally curious about love, but since I was young, my curiosity has centered around what it felt like, not what to call it. Perhaps some part of me has always understood that un-defining love is the only way I might actually get to experience it.

Growing up, my experience with relationship left me feeling fundamentally misunderstood. My friendships were intimate and comfortable. I was so fiercely loyal to my mentors that I left my parents and peers at a loss. I liked the idea of future-romance and looked forward to falling in love when I was older, but the idea of being romantic in the for real, right then, gave me the heebie-jeebies. I found the thought a little repulsive, in fact. My nearly thirty years of virginity hadn't been an expression of a hard-fought principle but of my nature. As a kid, I became aware that I seemed to be lacking this basic compass called 'sexual desire.' This tool was potent enough to provide my peers direction in their romantic pursuits and clarity of identity in the world. I marveled at the way it allowed them to so easily claim their categories of romance and relationship. I felt far too adrift to play with these permeant monikers.

In high school, my lack of interest in dating and boys inspired the L word to be thrown around often enough. In the 1990s, being gay still felt new and edgy. Most of us Midwestern kids only had reruns of *The Real World* as a point of reference. I wasn't allowed to watch *The Real World*. I imagined at times it would have been easier if I simply had been gay. At least I'd be defined. I'd 'make sense' to people. But, alas, I felt no more desire to kiss girls than boys. Even if I had been growing up in today's high schools full of gender rainbows and sexual spectrums, I don't know that I would have found much relief because it all still would have hinged upon categorizing and tagging love.

Fast forward, now, to 2014. I was thirty and pregnant, and *still* I didn't recognize myself in any of the myriad of recently minted relationship constructs or sexual pairings. *Still* I failed to fit in. *Still* the way I approached love was chronically misunderstood by those around me. And my failure to claim my category was all the more profound for the sheer number of labels now available to me.

That day I sat my parents down to tell them I was pregnant I saw just how strongly our socially sorting nature runs. Despite the fact that I'd consciously neither defined nor discussed my affinity, or lack thereof, to any category of sexual pairing, my family still had come to some strong conclusions. I had never proclaimed myself gay, never dated a woman, yet it took a nearly immaculate conception to break my own mother's brain of how it had sorted me. The experience was reinforcement of a warning I'd sensed my whole life: Define at your own risk.

This is not easy wisdom by which to live. Our desire for belonging is a formidable force. Stumbling across a definition in which we recognize ourselves is as much exhilarating as it is confining. There came a day when I finally stumbled across a experience of sexuality that seemed to resonate with my own. In that moment, some part of me leapt with joy at the recognition, thrilled to finally be seen. There was an immense sense of connection. The part of my being that longed to find community and safety and build social connections so that I'd be less likely to starve or be eaten by a saber tooth tiger—something primal in me—let out a whoop at the prospect of having found my tribe. I felt an un-self-conscious consequence-less impulse to announce to everyone immediately, "I am not a freak! I am not the only person on this planet having this completely anomalous experience! I'm okay, guys! I've found my category. I'm sorted."

That feeling lasted about .005 seconds before the backlash arrived, a thrashing, caged lion voice that roared, *You don't know me. Don't box me in!* Owning this label to another person meant concretizing in their minds who I was, how I behaved, how I would *always* behave. It would give them the right to call me out as duplicitous or mistaken if ever I felt or said or did something that fell out of alignment with this self-proclaimed identity (which I inevitably would, for no label can be all-encompassing of individual nuance). These new thoughts threw me into terror. My eyes flitted back and forth as though simply thinking this new self-definition too loudly had somehow leaked it into the ether, irreversibly subjecting me to everyone's scrutiny. My impulse to belong and the desire to be free felt at odds. So, I put the label to the side and remained in the inquiry.

Conclusion:

Life is our Love Laboratory. It is the lab in which we run our experiments and discover how and who we might be in relationship. And never have we more needed to tackle this grand experiment we call love.

Romance and sexuality used to need very little sorting. Heterosexual pairing off was the socially acceptable form of coupling. Period. Then around my parents' generation Western society began acknowledging a kind of binary system of straight and gay. Simple enough. Now in my generation, in an attempt to expand our understanding and articulate that love is not just one thing, dozens if not hundreds of new non-hetero-normative categories have been coined. From there we've seen each of these different categories blossom into its own spectrum, meaning that now there are literally an infinite number of places a person could fall on one of dozens of continuums and still manage to find themselves neatly tagged and sorted.

Evolutionarily we're hardwired to find the shorthand understanding of those around us so we can quickly and instinctually assess our safety in any given situation. *Predator, prey, friend, threat, family, tribe, potential mate, potential competition for a mate.* We love a good definition because they keep us alive and thriving.

The flip side of that efficiency is our brains' tendency to check the 'done' box once a categorization has been found. Once we've tagged a person, there is no longer a need to re-evaluate. To reassess someone every time we met them would be inefficient. For this reason, a proclamation of identity should be taken on with great caution. *We* may know that our declarations carry an implicit 'for now,' but our listeners' ancient brains likely hear 'forever.' (Don't believe me? Think about that one time you mentioned you liked purple when you were five, and your aunt gave you something purple every birthday for the next thirty years).

It is to you I am writing, my fellow un-defineds, you defined-for-nows, you want-the-option-to-change-your-mind, my fellow explorers and experimenters. If we want the freedom to be malleable, to change direction as new data comes in, we should be slow to self-label to the world because it takes an immense amount of energy to overcome the inertia of another's now set understanding of us. I hope (and believe) that definitions of romantic and sexual identity are getting so specific at such an increasing rate we'll soon be able to recognize the commonality of our individuality. Then we can get back to just calling love, 'love.'

Run Your Own Experiment No. 1:

The purpose of this experiment is to establish the facts of how we are perceived so that we can more consciously choose our behavior in relationship.

Experimental Procedure

1. At the top of a piece of paper, write the header *How Others Define [Your Name]*.

2. Set a timer for four minutes.

3. Complete this sentence as many times as you can before the timer goes off:

   [Your Name] is ____ the definition someone else holds of you. ____

   Do not stop your pencil, do not edit, do not consider, just write as fast as you can. It can be catalyzing to imagine specific people from all realms of your life and how they might answer that question.

4. When time is up, review the list and circle any definitions you resent or find displeasing.

5. For each circled trait, write a list of ways you have allowed or encouraged that definition of you to persist through your behavior, language, silence, etc.

Bonus Steps

1. For each circled trait, identify individuals who you believe hold that definition of you. (You might take note whether the same name comes up repeatedly.)

2. Choose one of those individuals who holds a displeasing definition of you.

3. Take a first step to disprove their definition. For example:

   a. Recommend an intellectual article to that man who defines you as an air head.

b. Show up five minutes early to a movie date with your girlfriend who defines you as chronically late.

c. Pick up the check at lunch with that co-worker who defines you as cheap.

d. Do something kind for that girl at school who defines you as a witch.

CHAPTER TWO

Track Your Unique Data

da·ta /ˈdādə/:
facts & statistics collected for reference or analysis;
quantities or characters on which operations are
performed, stored, and transmitted

SUBJECT: Overthinker; Female; Age 17 years, 2 months, 1 day.

HYPOTHESIS: Despite having a highly rational mind, I assume, based on observations of other adolescents of my species, that upon the inevitable engagement of the biological mating imperative, I will go completely insane.

METHOD: Advice, ambush, androids.

FIELD SITE: The high school jungle of the Midwestern plains.

Experiment 010.91.2:

The first time I saw *Star Trek: The Next Generation* I immediately recognized Data as my spirit animal. His was the voice that lived in my head. The gold-skinned android's open curiosity about human behavior and his plain direct questioning as he attempted to understand the motivations and emotions of those around him gave language to my own wonderings. Growing up, I experienced the world in a way some might call analytical, rational, cerebral, all labels that point towards the single fact that I wanted the world to make sense. I was compelled to understand why things happened the way they did. A clear 'if a then b' explanation provided me a deep sense of satisfaction. Alphabetizing the books on my shelf, sorting spreadsheets, color-coding my closet, roaming the Container Store, these things soothed me.

I reveled in order of any sort. In my teens I developed a quiet fantasy of becoming either a nun or a soldier. Both allowed me to luxuriate in thoughts of walking away from the chaos of my high school hallways and slipping smoothly into a world of order and regimen rigorous enough to appease my bone-deep craving.

Not surprisingly, I thrived in the classroom, a place of patterns and formulas, a place where expectations and deadlines were clearly laid out by adults, and I was allowed to deliver exactly above and beyond them. I was known as a nice girl, both athletic and artsy, so I got on well with my peers. Sophomore year I made a trio of best friends who embraced me and made my quirks feel nearly normal—in most realms, that is. When the topics of conversation turned to dating and sex, which it did more and more frequently as we got older, it was like trying to survive the football unit in gym class. I did my best to mirror what everyone else was doing and use the correct jargon, but ultimately it was still just me running around blindly, avoiding the ball until someone blew a whistle and told me I could change back into my normal clothes and resume my previously pleasant day.

I mean, I got that someday I was going to have sex with my husband—a part of me even looked forward to reaching that level of intimacy and trust with another as an adult—but the thought of it now, in reality, was just so...*weird*. I didn't understand why I had to even think about it at all until I was married. Whatever playbook everyone else seemed to have hardwired into their brains had not been hooked up upon my arrival to this planet. Dating, as far as I could tell, was a game with inscrutable rules. I began to see that whatever gene it was that flipped the switch to make teen-aged girls boy-crazy hadn't come factory standard in my body model. While my contemporaries seemed fixated on what it meant that the boy they liked had chosen to sit in the seat just in front and to the right of them rather than two rows back and to the left, I was obliviously taking the seat front and center in hopes of being noticed by the object of *my* adoration: the teacher.

Ironically, it was this natural lack of physiological entanglement that made me the go-to friend for dating advice. It appeared that logic was not an ingredient included in the soupy chemical marinade that saturates love-struck brains, so a little straightforward blunt analysis of a situation could easily masquerade as wisdom:

Sample 1

Suzie: So, he gave me this look in chem the other day that made me totally blush. And then in the hall just now he asked me if I wanted half of his Kit Kat. I mean, c'mon, he totally likes me, right?

Me: He's dating Amy, right?

Suzie: Yeah.

Me: Do you want to, like, fool around with him, or do you want to be his girlfriend?

Suzie: Oh, totally his girlfriend. C'mon, I mean…I would never be the other woman!

Me: No, hey, totally. <emphatic nodding> He *clearly* likes you. *Kit Kat-caliber* likes you. So, now all we have to do is find out whether he *girlfriend*-likes you or just on-the-side-likes you, and that's easy! If he doesn't break up with Amy and keeps sharing his Kit Kats with you, we'll know he is trying to fool around. But if he breaks up with Amy, then you'll know he wants more.

Suzie: <eyes wide> Oh my gosh, totally! That makes so much sense!

Sample 2

Jenny: He keeps saying that if I really loved him I'd smoke with him. That it's this thing we could share. But it's just so gross.

   Me: Do you still want to date him?

   Jenny: Totally. Like, for-*ever.*

   Me: Does he feel the same way about you?

   Jenny: He said, 'I love you,' while we were TPing Sandra's house the other night.

   Me: Oh my gosh, Jen-*ny*! You didn't tell me that! That's so sweet! Well, hey, then you have nothing to worry about. If you don't want to smoke, tell him you don't want to smoke. If he loves you, it'll be fine.

   Jenny: You're right. Yeah. <adamant nod> I'm just going to tell him I don't want to. <hesitation> It's just…what if he breaks up with me?

   Me: If what he meant by 'I love you' was 'I love you, but not as much as I love my cigarettes,' that would be totally lame. Honestly, you'd have confirmation that he's insane because you're amazing, and anyone that dumb doesn't deserve you. You'd be better off.

   Jenny: I guess…

   Me: I mean, really. Do you imagine yourself married to this guy when you're 40 and still pretending you like smoking for him? <causal shrug> Or maybe you'll just die of lung cancer before then.

   Jenny: Ew! Geeze. You're right. Good point.

Sample 3

Lanna: I mean, I've been making out with him for three months now, but he hasn't told his friends we're dating. He's probably just being a gentleman, right? Like, he's protecting me from his gross friends. <consideration face> Maybe I should give him a hand job.

   Me: <spit take> Okay, maybe. *Or,* maybe you could tell him you're the kind of girl who only makes out with her *boyfriend* and see if he decides to make it official.

   Lanna: OMG, that's brilliant! How did you think of that?

I was thankful to be able to comfort my tortured friends, though it felt like the advice was always the same: You're an amazing person. Period. Stop thinking that you need to do something to convince a boy of that. If he doesn't already get it, wrong guy. You are not defined by a boy's attentions...especially not *that* boy! It didn't feel revolutionary, but self-esteem and an ability to see through the hormonal fog was in high demand.

What horrified me was the knowledge that I would necessarily find myself in this same predicament someday. Though I had felt no hint of it yet, observation of my peers proved that the pursuit of romantic partnership was predicated by a radical abandonment of logic. I lived with the dreadful knowing that on my way to the happy marriage I would one day have, I would first have to lose my mind. I consoled myself with the certainty that that day was still far in the future, that I had at least a few good years of clear-headedness ahead of me, and I was determined to make the most of them. In the meanwhile, I stayed on alert, tracking the approach of any potential smarts-sucking boys with a leery eye.

I made it all the way to my senior year before, amidst all of my intention not to, I ended up with a boyfriend. It was entirely by accident, and I was a reluctant party to the whole affair. Phillip and I were both on the competitive speech team, we sat next to one another at lunch, and he was cast as the lead in the play I was student directing. My radar laid dormant with him because he had a girlfriend, a sort of third circle friend of mine, so he wasn't a threat. We became fast friends. I felt a sense of ease around him. He was safe.

Until he wasn't. He took his usual seat next to me at the lunch table one morning:

"Hey, how was your weekend?"

"It was good. Emily came over and watched the football game."

"Oh, nice."

"We had pizza."

"Yeah."

"And ... then, you know, we broke up." Tuna sandwich half way to my mouth, I did my best impression of a deer in headlights. *If I don't blink he won't notice I'm still here.* "So…yeah…"

I launched in on a totally unrelated topic, nervously attempting to reroute our conversation, klaxons going off in my head as though a friendly ship had suddenly started firing. *Red alert! Man your battle stations!* We didn't even make it out of the lunch room before Phillip suggested we date. "But you *just* broke up with Emily!"

"Yeah."

"Everyone's going to hate me because they'll think you broke up with her for me!"

"Yeah?"

"We have to let some time pass."

"Yeah."

He called me the next night. "I think we should date."

"But, Phillip—!"

"Yeah?"

Sigh. "Okay. Yeah. Fine." Phillip was my friend. He was a good person. And what was my excuse not to anyway? With the utterance of that defeated sigh, we were 'officially' boyfriend and girlfriend, and I began to mourn the death of my sensible, capable self.

Except I didn't change through my three-month tenure as girlfriend. I just stayed…me. I did (some) of the things I was pretty sure girlfriends were supposed to do, taking cues from both my friends and the latest chick-flick protagonist. Phillip and I held hands in theatre meetings and sat next to one another when our high school seniors group went to dinner at the usual spot. I liked having a go-to person in those situations. It made me feel sorted, a little special even. I continued to remain jumpy when he kissed me. It was just so, wet. What on earth did my friends see in making out? To me it felt more sloppy than sexy. When a group of us would head to my friend's house to watch movies, Phillip's hand would edge under my shirt and rest on the skin of my stomach. I didn't feel the need to protest. At times it even felt a little thrilling, though I was thankful that my friends faking sleep on the other couch guaranteed that his attentions would stay PG.

Through my foray into these foreign rituals I was surprised to find I remained the curious visitor rather than the fully immersed acolyte. Perhaps for this exact reason, Phillip recognized that I wasn't falling easily into the role of girlfriend. He called me one Saturday afternoon. I picked up the landline in my parents' bedroom in search of some privacy and held the phone to my ear. I sat cross-legged in a reading chair with my half-snoozing dachshund watching me from the floor with disinterested eyes. "Hi! What's up?"

It was a short conversation, ending with the mutual conclusion that we should no longer be dating. I knew the colloquial term was "breaking up," but it was all very calm and not at all what I thought a standard-issue break up was supposed to sound like. I'd always imagined that they required tears and pleas and in particularly exciting cases, lots of yelling and throwing things. It appeared that level-headed Logic had stuck around through my first break up as well.

When I hung up, the feeling that washed over me was unmistakable. I was relieved. I was grateful to have weathered an entire three months of being a girlfriend having held onto my rational reasoning. So much so that I almost didn't notice the slight tug of wondering whether I'd missed something.

Data Analysis:

Star Trek's Data was a feat of science so advanced that he couldn't be replicated. He was pure logic, computational power, and physical strength. But Data's deepest desire, like Wall-E or the Tin Man before them, was to experience human emotion. To someone who dreamed of an orderly existence, I never understood this eagerness to introduce a variable so volatile and clouding as emotion into what was an otherwise perfectly clear-eyed experience of the world. (If you're a sci fi nerd like me, you might remember that my skepticism was vindicated on star date 44085.7 when the U.S.S. Enterprise discovered an emotion chip prototype. When the chip was inserted, the experience was so overwhelming to Data's system that the it fused to his positronic brain. In short, he went temporarily insane. *See! You silly android! The grass is* not *always greener.*)

Like so many of us who live in our rational brains, I was certain from watching everyone around me that romantic relationship would prove to be my emotion chip. And unlike Data, if I became dysfunctional, there would be no Starfleet to step in and restore my systems. When my ability to think clearly was not destroyed by unreliable input tainted by hazy love emotions, I was thrilled at my luck, thrilled that I had somehow escaped the fate of everyone else around me. However, in that moment of confirmed 'otherness' I had to also accept that my relationships might be odd. I began to suspect that there were things on this planet that weren't going to come as easily to me as pattern recognition nor as elegantly as a mathematical proof. I was forced to consider whether the fictional android and I had more in common than I had ventured to imagine.

In the absence of a 'normal' emotional system I, like Data, became curious. I became scrappy, doing my best to understand intellectually the things that everyone else seemed to just 'get' on a physiological level. Don't get me wrong, I still witnessed what dating did to my friends with a touch of horror, but now that I knew it was not a thing I might not so easily experience myself, my observations became slightly more earnest. Because, while eventually, Data did learn how to integrate and modulate his human emotions so that he was able to straddle the best of both worlds, turning his emotions on and off depending on the needs of the situation, I suspected that my situation would not be so straightforward a fix.

Conclusion:

Each of us must track our own unique data in the Love Lab. There's no class in middle school that sits us down as kids and explores the nuances of what falling in love might look like. We all just kind of go at it vaguely guided by societal templates and sheer instinct, and when our experience doesn't match that of those around us or the screens in front of us (and it rarely does), watch out. This dissonance confirms, in our own minds, that we are weird, alien, broken. Some of us hide these deformed parts, others become defined by them, brandishing their different-ness with a defiant fist. Most of us dance some nimble combination of the two.

Entering the Love Lab has the unique ability to magnify these 'wrong' bits exponentially because partnership, by definition, requires the involvement of a second weird, awkward, slightly broken member of Homo (genus) Sapiens (species). It's one thing to know we're weirdos experiencing the world unlike anyone else, cloaked in a tapestry of fake-it-till-you-make-it. It's another thing entirely to give another person—a person we are certain must be way more well-adjusted than we are—a peek under the blanket and risk being recognized publicly as the freak we know ourselves to be. It is the risk required of us, however, if we are to ever experience the magic moment of encountering someone who desires to understand rather than condemn our weird and wacky perspective on the world.

While engaging with a lab partner has the potential to accelerate our self-understanding, the fabulous truth is that we don't have to wait for someone else to come along and reveal our broken bits to us. If we are able to suspend, for a moment, our self-condemnation and instead become curious, worried less about how our experience is *different* and more about how it *is*, we become true scientists of the Love Lab. It allows us to undertake a self-investigation, observing and collecting the data of our responses, reactions, thoughts, and beliefs which allow us in turn to begin to pinpoint our special abilities, our unique take on things, our secret superpowers. It lets us begin to speak our experience into the world so that our kindred, our tribe, stuck and isolated in their own similar-different experience, can recognize us, can be called into community, into partnership, and feel equally understood. Our claiming of our unique experience is an act of charity to those around us. So, get to know it, get to value it, and let that freak flag fly.

Run Your Own Experiment No. 2:

The purpose of this experiment is to establish the facts of the parts of self we consider strange so that we can choose connection rather than separateness within relationship.

Experimental Procedure

1. Answer this question: How many times have you been in a significant romantic relationship? (If your answer is zero, consider your deepest experience of relationship.)

2. For reference, write down the names of the people you've included in this count.

3. Now, take inventory of your <u>consistent</u> experiences over the arcs of these relationships, including their endings, by writing your answers to the statements that follow.

    a. In <u>all</u> of these relationships I felt physically _____ _____. *(ex. vigorous, turned on, nauseous, exhausted, attractive, etc.)*

    b. In <u>all</u> of these relationships I behaved _____ _____. *(ex. as a caretaker, as a child, as a cheerleader, as an insecure version of myself, as a stronger more capable version of myself, etc.)*

    c. In <u>all</u> of these relationships I thought _____ _____. *(ex. about our future, obsessively, of her whenever something funny happened, etc.)*

    d. In <u>all</u> of these relationships I experienced emotions of_____. *(ex. anxiety, happiness, excitement, confusion, etc.)*

4. Once complete, mark which thoughts, behaviors, and emotions you consciously or unconsciously hid from your partner.

5. Consider these questions:

    a. Why did you keep these experiences to yourself?

    b. What did you think expressing them would say about you as a person?

    c. Can you imagine a situation in which these aspects of your experience were recognized, incorporated, and valued?

6. Hold onto this list for use in a future experiment.

CHAPTER THREE

Live for the Disproved Theory

the·o·ry /ˈTHirē/:
a set of accepted beliefs or organized principles that explain and guide analysis; an idea that is presented as possibly true but is not proven to be true; the general principles or ideas that relate to a particular subject

SUBJECT: Overthinker; Female; Age 24 years.

HYPOTHESIS: Now in adulthood I have never gone on a date. Given that dating is a necessary step in mate finding, turning to methods that aid and support the dating process will increase the likelihood of finding my mate.

METHOD: Pencil skirts, 5-inch heels, heavy use of algorithms.

FIELD SITE: A collection of first-date-approved restaurants throughout coastal Southern California region.

Experiment 080.10.1:

It had always been a given in my mind that I would get married someday. It's just what my people did—both sides of my family, Midwesterners, church-going girls, strong attractive breeding stock—all of the clubs to which I held gold star membership. Plus, life with love just seemed preferable to the alternative. Yet, aside from my accidental three months with Phillip, I'd never felt inspired to date. As I neared my mid-twenties, inching ever closer to what had been modeled as a 'normal' age to get married, the practical voice in my head sat me down and gave me a stern talking to. *It's all well and good to talk about how great arranged marriage seems, but it certainly doesn't look like anyone's going to be doing the leg work to sell you off with a dowry anytime soon. If you want this to happen, you're going to have to get off your butt and start looking, kid!* I heeded this internal self-chastisement and did what any rational person would. I did the math.

Thirty felt like a nice time to get hitched—justifiably older than the norm so as to satisfy my desire to feel independent and worldly, not so young as to feel naïve of adulthood, not so old that the only available men would be divorcés or those who had something so wrong with them that everyone else had passed. So, that gave me, say, six years to accomplish the following:

- » meet a man
- » date a respectable amount of time (1-2 years)
- » be certain that I indeed wanted to marry him (~1 year)
- » get engaged
- » plan a wedding (1+ years)

So, I probably needed to meet that person in the next three or four years. *Okay, that's doable.*

Now, the actionable part. If I was going to meet someone and fall in love, I was actually going to have to get out of my house and meet some guys. I didn't feel excited by the thought of dating. In fact, it felt like a chore, but I had to respect the equation. If the probability of eventually being married (M) equaled the number of spouse-suitable men (S) divided by the total number of men I was willing to meet (T), then M = S/T. No matter how I worked it, if the total number of men I was willing to meet was 0, my prospects of becoming a spouse also came to nil. So, in support of my 5.7-years-future-self, I began the search for my eventual inevitable husband by turning to the ultimate mathematical algorithm: Match.com.

If you've ever done any online dating, you know that the process of creating a profile is confronting. It forced me to plainly define both who I was and what I wanted in a partner, questions I didn't often submit myself to so boldly. As I completed, tweaked, and totally reassessed my profiles through the next three years of mate-searching, I found the process got easier and easier. Each time I refined my definitions and desires, better informed by the previous cadre of dates. I got really good at it. (I was the first of what became many of us to venture into what was, at the time, the new and unknown land of online dating—what my girlfriends' saw as admitting defeat in their own prowess to go out into the real world and attract a man, I reassured them was simply a logical sorting of the wheat from the chaff.) Not only did I start writing my friends' profiles for them, but I also honed in on what I was actually looking at in a guy's profile (religion, height, employment), as well as what I had to offer (smarts, well-traveled, a cute bikini shot).

In fact, there was only one question that consistently gave me pause through the countless revisions. 'Wants kids?' I'd never felt 'yes,' but I feared that made me seem cold or unloving. The procreation urge simply hadn't seemed to switch on for me. As I saw it, this actually relaxed a lot of the pressure around finding a mate—both my own 'deadline' and the age range of the men I was open to dating expanded hugely without the viable-for-baby-making constraints— but, through each updated iteration of my online persona, I continued to leave that single answer lamely ambiguous. 'Not sure.'

I became a well-oiled dating efficiency machine. I determined that by signing up for three-month stints I could meet all the acceptable candidates in my surrounding zip codes. Then I needed to jump off long enough (another three months) for the new hopefuls (fresh meat) to join. I quickly dispensed with the long back and forth chats; I had more important things to do than discover over the course of a month that a guy had a cat named Tim and could cook spaghetti. I began suggesting we meet live in our first correspondence.

It went like this: once a guy reached out, I'd give his profile a quick once over and then email back offering to meet for dinner. The type of guy I'd reply to (Christian, gainfully employed, taller than 5'6", from the Midwest a major bonus) was so stunned, used to the site's usual clientele of cautious women not wanting to come on too strong, that they nearly always agreed to meet within the next 48 hours.

I found I was amazing at first dates. I was the rock star of first dates. I can only guess that it was because I showed up genuinely interested in finding out about these guys, and they seemed to find this flattering. I wasn't sure why, after all, don't you have to find out about someone to know whether you actually want to spend more time together? I mean, I was interviewing for the position of future husband, here! Why inefficiently waste time playing coy?

The boys I met (I still referred to them as boys which, even then, I suspected was telling) were all so sweet and earnest and nice. When we'd go out to eat about 60 percent would pay for the meal, 40 percent would go Dutch (a curiosity I attributed to being in Southern California. No one was splitting the bill back where I grew up in the Midwest). Some even planned thoughtful little first dates based on the interests I'd listed in my profiles. (The first time that happened I immediately logged onto my profile and deleted canoeing, roller coasters, and gardening from the interests section). Out of forty some-odd dates only 1 was strange enough that I hastened my departure before dessert, and even that guy texted me that evening asking when I was free to go out again.

Nearly every guy I went out with wanted a second date. Most reached out literally moments after we'd parted ways. I felt kind of bad about it, actually, because as easily as I jumped into first dates, it was rare that I was interested in a second or third. I simply wasn't attracted to any of them in that fluttery way I was supposed to be. Even when I expanded my age range and started going out with men ten and twelve years older, I would still leave feeling that between the two of us, in an apocalyptic *Independence Day* type scenario I would be the one fighting off the aliens while he stood back and earnestly cheered me on. I hadn't yet met the person that made me feel anything akin to being swept off my feet. Heck, by that point I'd have been happy to feel even a Saved By the Bell style flutter, the kind that passed between Kelly and Zack while holding hands over after-school shakes, inducing off-screen "ooooo's" from the live studio audience.

By the time I signed up for what would be my fifth and last round of online dating I was twenty-seven and a full-fledged mercenary. My parameters had shifted (religious-ish, gainfully employed, taller than 5'10", West Coast transplant a bonus). I took on just a one-month membership and blitzkrieged the situation. Over the course of three weeks I set up ten dates. I scheduled each of them for dinner on a weekday so I could meet the matches straight from work. This tactic was two-fold:

1) I was working at an insurance firm at this point, and I wore pencil skirts and 5-inch heels to the office everyday (thus the height requirement increase). This meant I looked sexy librarian hot, and meeting straight after work eliminated any need for think-about-what-to-wear energy or concern that they'd think I was trying too hard and had dressed up just for them.

2) I didn't want dating to spoil my weekend.

And if I'm honest, by that point, I was dating for entertainment. Not my own, mind you, but my friends'. I had become a real-life reality show, and this final three-week marathon took it to a whole new level. I came home each night, wrote up my analysis of the date, and sent it out to a dozen hungry inboxes. The reports went something like this:

Welcome all to the second week of Kristen's Crazy Dating Life (aka Making Up for Lost Time...)

BACHELOR NUMBER ONE: Allen

He's 25, a structural engineer for the state. He's a big guy—6'1" (yay!) and a churchgoer. He owns a house up in his hometown up North, and the two renters there right now are basically covering the mortgage (you all know how I feel about owning property...). He totally kept up with me in conversation without it feeling forced (amazing!). Generally, a nice guy. So that said, the important question:

DO I WANT TO MAKE OUT WITH HIM?: I can see that happening. He is definitely a guy's guy, and there is something attractive in that. Sure...I can see the appeal...

BACHELOR NUMBER TWO: Matt who "works for the Ritz-Carlton"

He had to cancel b/c his car wouldn't start. I then called bachelor 5 to see if he wanted to fill in, but he had just left for SF. Went home and slept.

BACHELOR NUMBER THREE: Chris

So you may notice that this update is coming a bit later in the evenings than the others. That's because I just walked in the door not too long ago...

The first impression was "cuuute..." when he came up to me. Of course, he was wearing scrubs. He's 30, has a great job as a med supply rep. He's got 3 siblings in the area, he's out in Simi Valley but is in Ventura 2-3 times a week, and we had great conversation. He grew up in Cali, but was a White Sox fan growing up (what are the odds!!!?) He's a total gentleman—bought my dinner, walked me to my car afterward. He has also taken a totally circuitous life path to end up in his current work, so we bonded over that.

At the end of the night he just said, "So, I am seeing you on Saturday, right?" to which I replied, "Yes, of course you are." Yes, ladies, I didn't even blink before giving up a night of my no family, no talking, no obligations weekend...I know!

DO I WANT TO MAKE OUT WITH HIM?: Well, he sort of kissed me. It was impulsive, but sweet and chaste...so...um...yeah.

From: Kristen Smith
Date: Mon, Sept 20, 2010 at 10:27pm
Subject: This Week's Installment of Matching!

First thing's first: UPDATE

I went on a second date with Chris on Saturday afternoon, and I don't know if it was me, him, the weather (which suuuuucked in Ventura), or the fact that I had changed my schedule from alone time to socializing time, but I found myself a little bored. I know! Bummer.

Now, on to what's on the fire for this week:

Can You Hear the Drums, Fernandoooooo?

He has an ABBA song about him, Lady Gaga gives him a shout out in her latest diddy, but neither of them has ever met the real... Fernando!

Okay...let me preface this with a conversation about flowers. Bringing a girl flowers is some sort of thing we're supposed find very sweet and romantic. I've had 3 guys bring flowers for me to a first date, and every time it's just made me feel awkward— like, what do you do with them? Bring them into the restaurant with you? Put them on a chair or the table? They just become this cumbersome prop that scream to everyone "I am on a blind date!!!" Am I totally alone in this?

If you haven't gathered, Fernando brought me flowers. It was, however, the best flower experience I've had. We met outside of the restaurant, we did the smiles, the enthusiastic hi, the hug, the flower pass, and some woman sitting in her car a few feet down started applauding! She was hollering about what a great greeting it was and that we should have fun and if I didn't want him she'd take him—it got us laughing!

So he's really quite good looking, and then on top of that he was in a starched shirt and tie (awesome!) and was super gentlemanly. There was an element of that guy who's too old for his age (he's 29)—like he missed being irresponsible and impulsive, and I could tell he didn't do this dating thing much. There was that feeling under it all that he was trying to sell it a little harder than absolutely necessary, but in an earnest way more than an annoying way. It was totally the most efficient date I've ever been on—there was no wasted time—we were in and down and up and out in a little more than an hour! I think he's better at his work (he's an engineer) than naturally relating to people.

DO I WANT TO MAKE OUT WITH HIM?: He is certainly a handsome guy, but I can't really imagine any sort of groping situation just yet...

As you may have already guessed, at the end of this month-long blitz, I did not find myself on my way to marrying Fernando nor Chris nor any of the other boys who crossed my path. Now twenty-seven, I'd asked myself more than a few times while preparing to leave for a date, "Why am I doing this?" The answer—to find a husband—was so evident though, that it wouldn't even entertain argument. If I was going to be married, I had to date. So, I bucked up, kept my head down, and soldiered on.

As I watched my dating subscription expire for the fifth time, I observed that I was no closer to marriage than I'd been three years earlier. Looking at the data, I had to allow for the emerging possibility that I might not hit my projected timeline for marriage. And then, a thought struck me. True, I couldn't argue with the math, but what if the *initial equation* was all-together erroneous? What if the solution *didn't* read = M?

What if it's not a given that I will eventually be married?

But I am 'the kind of girl who gets married.'

Am I the kind of girl who gets married?

Am I the kind of girl who wants to have a husband?

Do I want a husband?

I don't have a husband right now, and I like my life. I want for nothing. I have no biological clock ticking. I feel no lack.

Could it be that I'm the kind of girl who would be happiest <u>not</u> *married?*

WAIT, IS THAT AN OPTION!?

My excitement at this possible paradigm shift, that singledom wasn't a problem that needed solving gave me my answer. I suddenly felt as though I had been forcing myself to take medicine for a non-existent illness. Relieved, joyful, laughing in wonder at the abruptness with which my understanding of myself had completely changed, I deleted my dating profile then and there. I set about living my life by a new equation: $1 + 0^1$ problem.

Data Analysis:

"Do not be against anything." My favorite doctor of physics and scholar of both Eastern and Western religion Ravi Ravindra offers this wisdom to his students frequently. I've found it to be sage advice. The moment I mete out a mindless declarations of, "I would never wear yoga pants in public," or "I can't believe people bring their kids to this restaurant," or "It's just rude when someone answers their phone in the middle of a conversation," I can be assured that in no time I'll find myself cast in the role of a spandex clad mother of a rambunctious toddler who really—so sorry—just *has* to take this call.

So often we are unknowingly against the innumerable ways

love and romance might play out by virtue of being so stuck on the specific way we think it's supposed to happen. Despite indulging in fantasies of entering a nunnery, I'd always known I would get married. I was just 'that kind of girl. 'I was certain that a husband would appear on my doorstep one day who would make me feel all tingly, and, like so many other women, I would be thrilled the day he proposed, relieved to jump into our life together until death do us part. That's what was supposed to happen, and I never questioned it because it was simply a truth that lay someday in the future. What a surprise when 'someday' became 'someday soon' became 'now,' and it became quite apparent that the theory that I had been living under was proved incorrect.

You might be tempted to wave away those three years and forty-plus dates as a waste, but they were anything but. I couldn't have ever come to understand the kind of girl I *was* without finding out what kind of girl I *wasn't*. I had to go out and run the experiments, collect the data. The I-am-the-type-of-girl-who-gets-married theory had to be disproved if I was to make space for the possibilities of who I could be. Turned out I was not the kind of girl who felt tingly on a date with a man. Turned out, I was not the kind of girl who would be tidily married on a timeline. Turned out all those things I'd 'known' would just naturally happen because that's how the world worked for a girl like me, hadn't. I had been wrong about the kind of girl I was.

And when we come to that kind of realization, it is exhilarating! If we can be wrong about something so fundamental as the kind of person we are, how many other things might we be wrong about? The excitement of life is in finding that out.

Conclusion:

Be willing to be wrong about yourself. Be willing to be surprised. In the case of love, do not be against marriage, do not be against single, do not be against finding love very young or quite old, do not be against intimacy or sex or commitment or men shorter than you or women who can't cook, or anyone or thing that doesn't fall within your vision of what love and partnership will look like for you someday. Do not be against any of it, and you'll be less likely to run into your own limiting blind spots. Discover your preferences by actually testing them rather than blindly predicting them.

And do not be against yourself. Any aspect. Listen to the data coming in from your entire team of internal scientists. That part of you that finds yourself attracted to the bartender even though you have your sights set on marrying an investment banker. That piece of you who daydreams sometimes about what it would be like to be married to your best friend even though you know that pairing isn't what either of you is looking for. That inkling that, even though you've proclaimed your whole life that you're just not built for commitment, perhaps marriage wouldn't be such a bad idea if it meant that you got to live the rest of your life with this particular person. If you pick and choose which data to discard and which to include in your conclusions, you're implementing faulty and biased method and procedure, and the entire undertaking is invalid. An experiment only holds the promise of arriving at a truth when the experimenter is willing to collect and analyze *all* of the results, not just those that are most convenient.

Form theories, yes. We must. We should. It is a useful tool, especially for an overthinker. Declare your theories to yourself boldly! And then return these theories to their natural state: questions. Hypotheses. Remind yourself that a theory, be it about yourself or the world outside, is merely a jumping off point, a place to start. The fun part comes after, the part where you get up, go out into the Love Lab, and run your experiments, the part where you seek to prove and disprove your theories with curiosity and gusto, where you discover what is true for you. That part is called living.

Run Your Own Experiment No. 3:

The purpose of this experiment is to establish how we define ourselves so that we can mindfully choose whether or not to abide by any limitations those definitions imply.

Experimental Procedure

1. At the top of a piece of paper, write the header: *Things I Know About Myself.*

2. Set a timer for 4 minutes.

3. Complete this sentence as many times as you can before the timer goes off:

   I am the kind of girl/guy who _____.

   Do not stop your pencil, do not pause, if you get stuck, keep writing even if it's *"I don't know, I got nothin', there's nothing coming to mind..."* until you are again writing sentences that answer the question. Write as fast as you can, and if you're still rolling when the timer goes off, keep going until you run out of juice. Here are some examples to get you started:

   a. *I am the kind of girl who only sings in the shower.*

   b. *I am the kind of guy who orders his scotch straight up.*

   c. *I am the kind of gal who gets road rage when stuck behind a Prius going thirty in the carpool lane.*

   d. *I am the kind of person people can rely on.*

   e. *I am the kind of man who will teach his son to play catch.*

   f. *I am the kind of girl who can drive a pickup truck in high heels.*

4. Once complete, at the top of a second piece of paper, write the header: *Theories to be Investigated.*

5. Under it, rewrite each sentence from your list as a question, replacing "*I am*" with "*Am I*".

6. Read this list aloud and witness any reactions, emotions, or resistances that arise within you as you hear each question.

7. When you come across a sentence that feels uncomfortable, ask yourself whether there are any implied limitations within this definition of self. (i.e. because I am the kind of girl who X, I cannot/should not Y.)

Bonus Steps

1. Review your limiting-self-definition-turned-theories one by one.

2. Put a star next to each one where the thought of busting the implied limitations by disproving the theory makes you smile or, better yet, gives you a nervous thrill.

3. Choose one of these and take the first step to disprove it today.

CHAPTER FOUR

Choose the Correct Growth Medium

growth me·di·um /grōTH/ /ˈmēdēəm/:
(*or culture medium*) is a solid, liquid, or semi-solid
designed to support the growth of microorganisms;
different types of media are required for growing
different types of organisms.

SUBJECT: Overthinker; Female; Age 26 years.

HYPOTHESIS: In platonic friendships I have always felt free to love fiercely and enthusiastically specifically because the threat of sexual complications is absent. This kind of platonic intimacy should logically be able to thrive in any context.

METHOD: A grown-up job, a diagnosis, HR meddling.

FIELD SITE: A non-descript anywhere-America office park filled with twenty insurance brokers averaging forty to sixty years of age.

Experiment 110.42.2:

From the neck down my body was trembling so violently that I could hear the jingle of my bracelets knocking into one another in the quiet room. Despite this fact I was able to keep my expression blank and, in a kind of defiance, hold eye contact with my boss as he continued to speak. "I understand you're still new to all of this, but Amanda has no excuse. She should have known better." *Known better than what?* My mind was feverishly trying to work out what he was talking about. I knew I was in trouble, but I hadn't yet worked out why.

I'd come into the office that morning as usual, in a great mood after spending another sweet evening with my friend Amanda's family. I'd woken up that morning to a quiet house, made coffee, and left just as she and the kids were getting up. Her husband would sleep for a few more hours having just gotten off shift. Amanda kissed me on my way out the door. "I'll see you at the office."

Her text had come in just a few minutes before her arrival at ten o'clock.

> AMANDA: Ray wants to see me when I get in. Something's up.

I stared at the words, not knowing how to respond.

> AMANDA: He's not happy. He's going to want to see you too. Don't be scared. Just answer his questions.

Scared? Questions about what? My pulse quickened, and the back of my neck prickled at her urgent cryptic warning.

> KRISTEN: What's going on? What's wrong?

Before she could respond Amanda blew past my desk without so much as a glance let alone our usual hello and flew directly to her office in the back. My desk faced Ray's fishbowl of an office. I watched him push a button on his phone and his lips move upon registering her arrival. *He has that look he gets when he has dirt. When he's about to stir the pot.* There was something else too. Irritation?

Anger? I jumped when Amanda's office door abruptly swung open. She approached the fishbowl with the steely look of a woman heading to the gallows. She pushed the glass door open and entered enemy territory. Whatever storm threatened was now underway.

I had started working at the insurance firm eighteen months earlier as an underwriter's assistant. When I'd arrived, I'd taken note of the tiny firecracker of a woman who worked in the boating division. Amanda was all fast energy and bright smiles. At thirty-eight she'd given birth to her fourth baby just six months earlier, though you'd never know it from her figure. The adorable family photos on her desk attested to good genes.

It had taken a few months of working in close proximity for us to inch towards one another. She told me later that I'd come across as all business the first few times she tried to engage, likely because I had no idea what I was doing working in insurance with an architecture degree and was trying to do a good job of convincing people that I was worth keeping employed. But I'd listen to her stories in the staff lunchroom with a kind of warm fuzzy fascination. Who was this woman with a successful career, four kids, a charmed marriage, and beaming joyful energy to spare?

Amanda's persistence finally broke through my self-doubt. We went out to lunch and connected immediately. It wasn't long before we began finding excuses to work together on projects, and I reveled in feeling useful to her. We had crossed beyond the line of mutual admiration and were toeing the waters of genuine friendship when her diagnosis came in. She had ALS. The disease was fatal and so rarely affected women, let alone women as young as she, that the doctors, in utter disbelief, spent months re-testing. Every one came back positive. Her oldest kid was just six. She was still breastfeeding the youngest. Her husband worked nights as a paramedic. She was the primary breadwinner. The doctors told her she had less than twenty-four months to live.

Amanda was facing a painful, ugly death, and perhaps solely

because of that fact, she threw caution to the wind and invited me in. She needed practical as well as emotional support from someone without baggage or need or judgment. As an unattached twenty-six-year-old who had no story about her and plenty of time and energy, I was perfectly placed to provide that. For the next three months I spent my evenings and weekends diligently studying how each of her kids liked their lunch (crusts on this one, grape jelly for her, strawberry for him), rearranging the contents of the kitchen cabinets (because she'd been meaning to get around to that for years), taking the kids to the beach, putting together photo albums with her late into the night over wine. We laughed, cried, grieved, and, of course, planned. We became sisters. We spoke freely and frequently of our love for one another, of the life-line we each were for the other, of the un-knowable perfection of fate's timing and our friendship.

Any fears I had about encroaching on her family time were assuaged again and again. Her husband was adamant that I stay and spend a lazy Saturday with them while the kids napped so that he and Amanda could properly educate me in the most important cinematic experience of all time: Top Gun. They trusted me with the children—notable because they'd never let anyone but family babysit before. On her one day a week working from home I would smile to myself as I received emails and texts from Amanda every few minutes, sometimes with purpose, sometimes just to say she loved me or say thanks, and often to ask when I was 'coming home.'

Eventually I was going back to my place only to sleep and occasionally do laundry. I arrived at her house one afternoon to find that she had converted the home office into a guest bedroom and cleared a closet for me. The kids excitedly showed me around "KK's room." Before long her three-year-old was in the habit of climbing into bed with me in the mornings so that Amanda could sleep a little longer. Though unspoken, it soon felt like she was instructing me in her world. She was instructing me so I could be of help when she was no longer here.

I was aware that I was in the midst of a defining moment of my life. I was completely devoted to not only my friend, but her family, to her children. I felt God had put me at this place at this time for a purpose. I was useful here, I was able to be a tool to relieve suffering. And in return, I was allowed to show up with all of my goofy intensity and love and enthusiasm and was met time and again with appreciation and validation rather than raised eyebrows and judgment. All of me got to show up and be seen and loved. It felt like a miracle.

As we became closer I watched Amanda pull back from many of her relationships. She would sometimes confess that she felt bad about it, but she just couldn't handle the looks, the questions, the invasiveness. The HR woman in particular seemed desperate to be a part of Amanda's tragedy, so we were quiet about our arrangement around the office. I reassured her time and again that she didn't need to feel bad about dropping people from her life, she needed to do what she needed to do. There was no usefulness in giving time to those who were just going to drain her waning energy. She was dying, for Pete's sake. She could do whatever she wanted.

Amanda was in Ray's office for over thirty minutes. Only low muffled tones escaped the reverberating glass when either spoke, and her stoic expression gave nothing away. I had no clues as to what was going on. A deep seated fear began to grow with each passing minute. I didn't know what we'd done, but it was clear we were in trouble. I was in trouble. By the time they'd finished and Amanda had retreated back to her corner, I felt ill, filled with adrenaline that had no opportunity for release. I almost welcomed the relief of finally hearing my name called, of finally being told what this was all about. Of finally releasing my leashed mind into action, into plans of how to fix it.

"Kristen, could you come in here for a moment?"

I nodded silently, not trusting my strangled voice. I calmly and purposely walked through the swinging glass door and took a seat on a leather couch that looked as though it'd been transplanted from a German bachelor pad for all its slickness and angles. I reflexively crossed my arms, and my legs followed as though my body was attempting to hold itself together. Taking Amanda's cue, I kept my expression cool, ignoring my body's rhythmic almost comical jerking as it began to shake. The still-nameless dread opened wider within me, a gaping sink hole giving way, threatening to swallow me up.

"Kristen, I got a call early this morning from the HR department in Seattle. They have been reading emails between you and Amanda. They have some concerns."

They've read our emails? I envisioned the woman down the hall pawing greedily through Amanda's email inbox, gleefully highlighting passages for review by the home office. My mind scanned, searching for anything I might have written that would jump out as a problem, as the thing I'd done wrong, but nothing popped. As far as I could remember nearly all of our back and forth was logistics and funny stories and general check ins with one another.

I tuned back into what Ray was saying, "…The sheer number alone is a problem." I flashed back to months earlier when I'd asked Amanda for her personal email address, and she'd told me she never checked it, she only used her work email for everything. At the time, I'd thought that unwise of her, and was kicking myself now for not being more persistent. Ray's mouth was still moving, but I wasn't registering his words. I felt like a little girl chastised for giggling as I huddled in the back of the classroom passing notes with my best friend. *All right, girls, break it up.* But all of this couldn't really be about us being too chatty, could it? I mean, Bob wasted half of the day wandering from office to office, cup of coffee in hand, chatting people up and distracting us from our work. Surely our electronic patter paled in comparison.

"…and they're not willing to be pulled into a sexual harassment suit…" That word pulled me out of my reverie. What was he *talking* about? *Sex* wasn't a part of this. If he read the emails he had to know that. We talked about how much we loved each other, sure, but we weren't having sex! I was with her *kids*, her *husband!*

"…I understand you're still new to all of this, but Amanda has no excuse. She should have known better." He delivered the next sentence as a command. "You two need to stop whatever is going on. You need to take a break from Amanda."

It was as though someone had taken all of the air out of the room. I was in disbelief. They couldn't do this, right? A company can't dictate who you do and do not see on your own time, can they? And I still didn't understand what I'd done wrong! I had a friend whom I loved. How was that a problem? How was that a threat to the company? How was it any of their business in the first place? I held my tongue both by design and in desperation. Even if I had wanted to protest, I wouldn't have known what to say. It would have been blindly shooting at a target only they could see. It was as though they were talking about our friendship—our sacred, life-giving, nourishing connection—like it was a tawdry office affair being had on company time. I was utterly baffled by the waves of shame, fear, confusion, and anger that rose within me.

When dismissed, I left his office resolute, already ticking off the ways that Amanda and I would have to change our patterns to keep our life together a better secret. When I sat back down at my desk, my phone buzzed with her text message.

AMANDA: We need to take a break.

I felt the hot painful prick of adrenaline flood my body. My eyes sharpened, my mind tunnel visioned as I kicked over into full fight or flight. Life or death. *No. Unacceptable. I cannot lose her.*

KRISTEN: Why? There's no problem here. We can handle this. I can still come over like we planned.

AMANDA: I need to go home and tell Rick tonight. I need to do it alone.

Tell Rick what? What had Ray said to her in there? Had they threatened her job? Could they do that? On what basis? I could feel myself panicking. I could feel a dark drop of poison blooming outward in the tranquil little sea we'd built together, and I felt powerless to stop it.

I didn't hear from her all weekend, and Monday she didn't come out of her office. Throughout the day my eyes wandered in the direction of her closed door, but I dared not go in. When five o'clock hit, I plodded out to the parking lot, weighted down by the pain of my uncertain future, the sudden boulder placed in the path to my purpose. I opened the driver's side door of my small two-seater truck and found piled in the passenger's seat a riot of clothes, books, shoes, a hairdryer, and pajamas. It was every last belonging I'd kept at Amanda's. And propped on top was a small jar filled with multi-colored sea glass. I identified it immediately as the sea glass I'd collected with her and the kids when they'd excitedly shown me their favorite beach for hunting it weeks earlier, all of us laughing in competition to find the rarest colors and biggest pieces. The message couldn't have been clearer: It's done.

I drove away from the coast on the winding mountain road that led back to my safe little valley town and considered how I'd again managed to stumble into trouble so unawares. I'd been constantly cautioned by my father growing up, "Kristen, know when to say when," as I too enthusiastically loved my sister or hugged the dog. I was a bouncing ball of affectionate enthusiasm that was simply inappropriate and, as my parents often had to remind me, 'too much' for most settings. I involuntarily winced remembering when, as a nine-year-old, I'd tagged a neighborhood girl with such zest that we collided, tumbling into the slick grass, still clinging to one another as we slid down the small hill of my front yard. I couldn't guess at the cause of her scream until we'd landed together at the bottom, and we could both see that the force of my enthusiasm had broken her arm. Nearly two decades later I still felt my stomach churn nauseously at the memory, so intense was the surge of shame that my blind, joyful, barreling forward had caused such unintended pain. Had I done this again? Had the way we'd moved into love with one another been exuberant, or reckless? Could I tell the difference?

But this is just how I am, I thought despairingly. *This is how I'm hardwired.* My mind conjured one of the countless photos of me as an apple-cheeked little kid, smiling so widely my eyes shut, squeezing another kid with all the might in my short chubby little arms. Sometimes the other child pictured was grimacing, trying to wedge an elbow between us. Other times they were squeezing me back wearing a grin to rival my own. As the dozens of selfies on my phone attested, Amanda had squeezed back.

If our relationship was a problem, then how I loved was a problem. I was a problem.

Data Analysis:

There is perhaps nothing more painful in the human experience than the feeling of being misunderstood. And when it happens to us in the context of a loving relationship, the pain is all the more severe. To this day, I still don't know the specifics behind the ending of my relationship with Amanda. The closest I've been able to guess is that the company read our emails as some sort of clandestine affair and threatened her job. Misinterpreted by a faceless entity on the other side of the country, our friendship had been identified not as the sacred, uplifting, healing relationship I experienced, but as an inappropriate, lascivious office romance. Outside forces had turned something I found life-giving and beautiful into something shameful and unspeakable.

The pain of not understanding the entire experience was all-encompassing. I didn't understand what corporate had thought happened. I didn't understand why my boss thought Amanda and I were in the wrong. I didn't understand how she could abandon me and our relationship, the relationship to which I felt completely devoted, so abruptly. So absolutely. I felt totally unmoored from my sense of what was and was not normal behavior and frightened that I didn't know how I had gotten here or how to keep myself from finding myself here again in the future.

Because sadly, this was not new territory for me. My natural physical exuberance and intense loyalty to those I claimed had always sparked some level of confusion in my parents, and they'd only grown more befuddled as I'd gotten older. As a child I'd been given leeway to kiss whomever I wanted, wrestle, hug, cuddle, nap with, hold hands with my friends anytime I was inspired by the joy of our connection to do so. I didn't understand why adulthood should change any of that. It felt insane that I couldn't play with my friends the way I used to just because some adult told me I was too old for it anymore. It was a dumb rule. And even worse, it was an ill-defined rule. I couldn't point to a clear distinction between who I could and could not share a hug or a bed with. So, I chose to reject the premise entirely.

What I hadn't understood was that there was a condition for relationship, one that I resisted or that I hadn't fully grasped in my still innocent mindset until experiencing the heartbreak of Amanda (and, rest assured, it was a heartbreak). It was the condition of context. Amanda and I had chosen a hostile environment. We worked together. We'd entered a free will agreement with an entity that gave us money in exchange for our labor. So, we agreed to play by their conditions, no matter how absurd. Amanda and I had sowed our relationship in fallow soil, in an environment that could neither support nor nurture it. Our only options were to watch the relationship die or to change the context by leaving the company.

I still embodied an exuberant child's understanding of boundary-less expression of affection, and it felt impossibly unjust that I was being told to change who I was just because someone misunderstood me. In fact, if I'm honest, there are some days that still feel that way. It's taken me many years and many more relationships to understand that part of being truly loving is recognition of the rules that others have chosen to live by; that it's not about changing who we are, but about being responsible in our awareness of social cues in the circles of which we freely choose to be a part. It's about respect. We always have the option to leave a tribe whose understanding of the world is too alien from ours. And indeed, not long after recovering from the loss of Amanda, I left the world of the eight to five corporate job in search of a different culture.

That's not to say that I always get my context cues right these days. Occasionally I'll retro-actively be forced to question whether I've crossed a boundary in light of an outsider's response. This happened not long ago when I was sharing a hotel room with my two tall, handsome, Australian rock-star former business partners at a conference in Cabo. It wasn't uncommon for someone to think I was married to one of them for the ease we had with one another, and the three of us, like siblings, thought nothing of sharing a room. Nor did either of the guy's wives who knew me and had themselves been on the receiving end of my mad hugging skills. But the strange looks and knowing comments of "lucky girl" from the event coordinators gave me pause. There was an implication of impropriety in their raised eyebrows and smirks. Had I yet again stumbled into an 'inappropriate' territory? Was I, despite my best efforts, unknowingly back in the land of weird and unusual behavior that could harm the very people I loved?

I did what I have now learned to do in these situations of uncertainty: I asked. I asked my partners whether I had missed something, whether there was any discomfort with the sleeping arrangement for them, for their wives, for anyone involved. Much to my relief, the guys waved these questions off as unnecessary. As they did to my follow up, whether I, in the petri dish of this conference, need to hide the fact that we were sharing a room? Because this I'd learned too from my time with Amanda and in subsequent relationships, if I simply hid my intimate relationships from prying eyes, I didn't have to feel I was doing something wrong. It was a practice I'd perfected over the years, but while I found it effective in protecting all involved, it did have one major downside. It left me feeling unseen, and my relationships feeling invalid and shameful. It reinforced that my style of love was less than, not quite worth acknowledgement or recognition. I learned I much preferred contexts that allowed my relationships to be fully expressed, that embraced me because of my enthusiastic embraces, not in spite of them. That is what I now seek.

Conclusion:

As in any successful experiment, for intimacy to thrive, the correct agar is required. Prime your petri dish with the correct growth medium, and it will find nourishment to blossom robust and healthy. Seed your intimacies in an agar that has been formulated to feed entirely contrary types of relationships, and it will only ever become thin and anemic, or perhaps worse yet, it will grow explosively, wildly, and then die without warning.

Approach cultivation of intimacy not as a defiant thorn on a rocky outcropping, determined out of spite and principle to exist in the harsh landscape no matter how miserable and difficult. Intimacy is the most noble of experiments, full of risk and requiring both bravery and tenderness. Be kind to yourself and your intended by setting your endeavors up for success. Give them every genuine chance of flourishing. Plant your sapling intimacies in rich soil and tend to them with care. You will still find that not all of your seeds will grow, but those that do will bear delicious fruit.

Run Your Own Experiment No. 4:

The purpose of this experiment is to catalogue our existent petri dishes so that we may more effectively engage them in experiments of relationship.

Experimental Procedure

1. On a piece of paper, write a description of a type of relationship you'd like to have (or have more of) in your life. Focus on how you and the other party would talk, behave, and express your closeness when you are together.

2. Write a list of all of the existing petri dishes in your life.

    (For example: the office, the gym, church, mommies group, the PTA, extended family, marriage, the classroom, etc.).

3. Review your description from Step 1 and put a star next to any petri dish you feel holds the correct growth medium for the type of relationship you seek.

4. Keep your eyes open as you move in those circles this week for new relationship opportunities.

Bonus Steps

1. Write a list of *potential* contexts that might support and nourish the relationship description. That is, petri dishes you do not currently access but in which you could imagine finding like-minded friends or partners. *(For example: acting class, the yoga studio, working mothers networking, a writer's circle, pick-up basketball, etc.)*

2. Choose your favorite one off of this list and take the first step towards connecting with that tribe.

CHAPTER FIVE

Follow the Biology of Desire

bi·ol·o·gy /bī'äləjē/:
the study of the physiology, behavior, and vital
processes of a particular organism or class of organisms.

SUBJECT: Overthinker; Female; Age 29 years, 11 months, 8 days.

HYPOTHESIS: Sexual attraction serves to focus a human beings'
mate-finding attentions towards suitable breeding partners. It follows
that this correlation would also work in reverse inasmuch that locating
a suitable mate should engage my biological desire.

METHOD: Coffee, kissing, dream analysis.

FIELD SITE: A carefully chosen couch, my regular yoga studio,
the theatre of my own mind.

Experiment 140.22.7:

I had been out with David a number of times over the past few
months, a phenomenon that likely occurred due to the fact that

being with him didn't feel particularly romantic. He was local, and perhaps because of that, was also the sole survivor from my final stint of online dating. In our first encounter, I mentioned that nun-hood was still at the top of my list of viable future career paths. He seemed to think this fact made me more interesting rather than less so, so I said yes when he asked me out again later that week. He was a good, kind, grounded man, and after a few weeks, I acknowledged that it wouldn't be a total disaster if I were to find myself physically attracted to him. We were similar ages, he was empirically attractive, taller and bigger than I which satisfied the ancient part of me that needed to know he could club a saber-toothed tiger if we came under threat. Yes, in fact, I could point to no reason that I shouldn't find myself desirous of David's sexual attentions. So, I kept my eyes peeled for any little internal ping or twinge indicating I was indeed aroused by his presence. None appeared.

I was nearly thirty, and though I had happily embodied the knowledge that I didn't need a husband, I was beginning to wonder if my lack of sexual interest was an indicator that there was something fundamentally screwy with my wiring. The mythic Biological Imperative I'd feared growing up remained a stranger to me, its species-propagation-driven ambitions seemingly satisfied to remain in an eternal state of slumber. But I was no longer a seventeen-year-old being spared sexual stirrings for an accidental-boyfriend. I was an adult now, and I had begun to consider that I might be missing out on a key part of the human experience.

Perhaps I just needed to prime the engine. Maybe I'd gone so long without revving it that it'd locked up on me. I tested this theory one morning when, after I told him I had a crazy day ahead of me, David thoughtfully showed up at my place with a cup of my favorite coffee. I pointedly kissed him in thanks. It was chaste, to be sure, but I was hoping it would be enough for a spark. At completion of the lip to lip Phase of Contact (POC), I scanned my body for data. Increased heartbeat? No. Flushing or sweating? No. Shifted breathing pattern? Only the evidence that I'd held in my coffee breath for the duration of POC. Conclusion: no arousal response indicated.

However, neither was there evidence of any negative fallout. So, two days later we kissed again at the end of a dinner. The POC was significantly extended this time and the lip seal breached resulting in co-mingled breathing patterns. The interaction was not unpleasant, but again I recorded the experiment as a null set.

Maybe kissing alone simply wasn't enough to get my particular motor running. Maybe I had one of those old-timey crank motors that need some serious elbow grease to turn over and start humming. I set to imagining how I might coax awake my hibernating passions. I'd spent a lifetime dreading the moment when some boy was going to walk by me, and I, captured by a sniff of his ineffable chemistry, became like a cartoon character floating towards the wafting scent of a freshly baked pie in a window; I'd make a halting U-turn to follow him, eyes bugged out, tongue lolling to the side, powerless and hungry, till death do us part. Well, it was time to start making the power of chemistry work for me. If only I could catch a whiff of those microscopic intoxicants, science told me they would obligingly strap me into my seat on the pheromone rollercoaster, and I could just sit back and enjoy a nice fat hit of dopamine while they went to work.

Perhaps my previous interactions with David had simply not been heated enough to trigger pheromone release. The next time David visited, I tested a new technique: a make out session. It was fun and light, and while he was clearly interested, he let me go at my own pace. It was, by all accounts, not un-nice. I found that the more athletic engagement—traversing from front door to kitchen to couch, regularly shifting positions among supine to prone to seated, negotiating one another's limb position and body weight—involved my whole body in such a way as to encourage many of the physiological responses associated with sexual arousal: sweat, flush, shortness of breath, and elevated heartrate. This direction of inquiry held promise! So, I was completely taken off guard when I saw David two days later, and I didn't want him to touch me.

The reaction, though delayed, was strong. The next time we went out I dodged his kiss, and I felt myself shirking away from the most innocuous physical touch. The outcome flew in the face of my initial hypothesis—not only had my attempt to spark sexual interest failed, but it had instead awoken some sort of repulsive force as though David and I were now two negatively charged ions. I observed the effect grow until a completely unfounded irritation arose within me anytime I so much as thought of him.

What a finding! This unforeseen turn made me doubly happy that I'd waited to test sexual desire with someone already established as a genuinely good person and viable mate. The certainty of that experimental parameter saved me from labeling my reactionary response as anything other than what it was: My Stuff. David was the constant in this equation. He was still a good guy. I just plain didn't physically desire this good guy. And, clearly, the part of me that felt I was ignoring that fact was now hell bent on convincing me to make him to go away. Recognizing what she was up to, I wasn't at the mercy of her pissed off opinions. In fact, I was grateful for her vigilant attempts to protect me from myself. *I'm sorry, you're right; now I know I can't force a physical relationship where none is indicated. I'll fix it.*

I asked David to lunch to share my findings and salvage the relationship that had been so pleasant just two weeks prior. "So, you see how I've come to conclude that some part of me just isn't interested in physical intimacy right now—sexual intimacy, to be specific. And, listen, you haven't done anything here. You're great. I so enjoy our conversations. This is My Stuff." Internally I winced as I heard these words emerging from my mouth akin to what television told me was the classic 'it's not you, it's me' speech. I was worried David would think it was a line, that I was merely sparing his feelings, but what could I do? It was true! "I think I must just be a slow burner. So, I'd like to just rewind two weeks, before that kiss, and pick up where we left off. Back when everything was fine. Maybe I just need more time."

David was, as always, patient and interested as he listened to me. I was relieved we seemed to be on the same page. As we stood in the sunshine in front of the restaurant and said our good-byes, I felt proud of us. I'd been honest, he'd been receptive, we'd talked through everything like mature evolved human beings. This had gone great.

David moved to leave but hesitated. I perked up inquisitively as he turned back to face me, "So, just one more thing," he asked, "... Were we dating? And are we breaking up?"

That evening I arrived at my yoga studio full of disquieting questions and expectant of answers. I was doing all the things I could think of to allow sexual attraction to show up, but clearly it wasn't working. The 'Who's on First?' conversation David and I had had as we parted had just made me feel even more like I was missing something fundamental. I kept replaying it in my mind, trying to glean clues.

David: Were we dating? And are we breaking up?

Me: Well, I mean, we're the same as we were…I talk about you as someone I'm seeing…

David: I just mean, I treat someone I'm dating differently than someone I'm not.

Me: <blank stare> How? <struggle face> You mean, like, logistically? Like, who pays for a date?

David: Well…sure. But I'm going to interact with the person I'm dating differently than I would my friend.

Me: <bewildered head shake> …I'm sorry, I'm not understanding…

The workshop I was taking that evening was being taught by Naomi who had become a close friend over the previous nine months. She began the session by asking us to set our intentions for our time together over the next three days of the workshop. I sat with my eyes closed, tucked in cozy atop two rolled yoga blankets. My whirring brain slackened its analysis of recent events and predictions of the future to join me in the now. I dropped into presence, my body landing in the space weighty and solid, my arms draping heavily over my legs. I felt my breath move in my nostrils. I drew my attentions inward, to the empty stage of my mind. Thoughts drifted in and out of the vastness, dancing through the cool air of the dim, cavernous space like dust motes riding invisible currents. For all the movement, this internal theatre was still. Then, BAM! A mantra appeared emblazoned across the empty stage in the form of a literal lightbulb-bedazzled marquee flooding the inside of my skull with blinding light. It spelled out a single word: DESIRE.

Over the last year I had been, correctly and necessarily, moving away from the misalignments within my life. Clearing out the things that I had mindlessly collected, ideas and definitions that weren't actually mine, that I didn't actually want, like a deep spring-cleaning of the soul. I'd worked hard to drop obligations both unnecessary and imagined, unhealthy relationships, attachments to who I thought I was supposed to be. I'd even left the safe, steady, soul-crushing insurance job and taken up yoga in the interest of chipping away at all of the things I'd built up through a lifetime unawares, having mistaken them for fundamental aspects of myself. Now, sitting in this studio, stripped down to the bare bones of being, I wanted to *want* again. I wanted a feeling of desire to arise and propel me *towards* my life. I wanted something to point me towards the joy.

My body buzzed with the certainty of it. I could feel clearly the desire for *desire* thrum through me with the pulsing of my blood, the rush of it in my ears. I managed to keep my eyes closed, but I gave the exhilarated smile that broke out blindly across my face free reign. My legs caught the urge to fidget, and it took everything I had to not leap up and fly out the door of the studio to immediately begin my mission, to put into action a life in the world guided by this simple and powerful directive: DESIRE.

The mental imprint of the marquee stayed with me through the evening's practice as Naomi guided our movements on the mat and in meditation. It hadn't faded by the final namaste. This new guiding principle felt exciting, and I left the studio energized, still feeling giddy and full of possibilities as I climbed into bed. Before drifting off I prayed for a dream of desire, something experiential to remind me what it felt like to want. It was a whimsical prayer. I wasn't one of those people who could conjure up the answers to their soul's deepest questions in the dream world—in fact, most nights I was barely able to remember my dreams—but I was feeling hopeful and playful, and why the heck not?

I'm sitting at my detective's desk at the police precinct. I'm finishing up a few last work items in excited butterfly-filled anticipation of the date I have at the end of the day.

"Hey! You got any big plans this weekend? Going out on one of those match dates?"

"Yeah, you are the mas-ta'! You go get 'em!"

My male colleagues punctuated their heart-felt if ill-expressed compliments with finger guns and winks so cheezy as to induce an eye roll. I laughed with them in proud acknowledgement of my reputation for loving and leaving 'em, "Something like that." I smile like the cat who caught the canary, giddy over my secret liaison. One of the other detectives I'd been earnestly pursuing for months had finally—finally!—said yes to a date. I drop my head to hide the grin lighting across my face at the thought. My entire being is thrumming with excitement for this chance to expand our relationship into uncharted waters. I know this is the start of something important. I know this is the first step towards collaboratively building a life with another. Our life, together. We have an entire weekend ahead of us, and I anticipate making good use of it.

I close my laptop and head to the women's locker room to change out of my work attire into something more special. My heart is thumping hard, and my eyes are bright in the mirror as I apply lipstick. I emerge into the hall to whistles and jocular cat calls from my brotherly co-workers. My eyes meet my intended's in a conspiratorial gaze. She raises an eyebrow, a corner of her mouth lifting into a smirk of acknowledgement as I make a slow spin to indulge the other detectives' calls.

"Niiice!"

"Yowza, this guy doesn't stand a chance!"

My laugh rings freely, "You know it, boys!" I sling my bag over my

shoulder knowing my intended's eyes will follow me out the door before she
sets down the file she's still holding, picks up her coat, and leaves to join me.
"See you Monday!"

My eyes shot open at 5:00 AM on the dot. Stone still in my bed, I stared blankly at the ceiling, replaying the dream, running my body back through the physical sensations of the experience, afraid that if I blinked I'd lose it. When I was sure I had the whole thing safely in my memory from beginning to end, I quickly took inventory of my physical status. Heart-rate high, chest flushed, lower spine arched, perspiration in evidence along hairline, breasts, and back, excitement present in the belly, longing constricting my chest, nervous fear congregating just beneath my scapula, and unadulterated joy permeating from the crown of my head to the tips of my toes.

This was desire. And it felt amazing.

I released the breath I'd been holding in one long rush. And then I laughed. I laughed and threw my hands over my face and shook my head in disbelief and amusement. *Seriously!?* That's *how you answer me?* I'd been delivered exactly what I'd asked for. The dream had provided a touchstone to feel into and embody the energy and possibility and forward momentum of desire. I could now cue up the physical experience of being swept into the excitement of moving towards a beloved. It just so happened that all of this was now accessible through the dream-memory desire for a woman.

Now, I've mentioned to you before that I'd often checked in with myself around the question of whether my disinterest in the men around me was an indication I was gay—it would have been irrational not to—but my lack of sexual attraction to men appeared to be rivaled only by my lack of interest in sleeping with women. The direct memory I now held from my dream made me a touch giddy though, nervous and exhilarated. I wanted to want someone, and I could feel an internal shift; I felt as though I had been truly opened to the genuine possibility of wanting either gender. The feeling of new possibility excited me. And such precise fulfillment of my prayer in this unexpected container made that opening feel sanctioned, intentional, like the Universe and I had an understanding. I laughed with the feeling that I had a giggly little inside joke with my BFF, God.

I was smiling as I shuffled out of my bedroom into the quiet kitchen and put on the kettle for coffee. Waiting for its whistle, I leaned against the counter. My eyes rested on the row of trees in the orchard beyond my kitchen window. Together we waited, the trees and I, they in their misty morning blues for their bath of neon yellow-green that would arrive with the sunrise. In the stillness, the synaptic connection that abruptly clicked in to place felt like a lightning bolt. It was followed by the thunder crack of comprehension as the required neurons came on line. Just like that I understood both what David had been asking me the previous day and why I hadn't understood him.

Most people are attracted to someone and THEN get to know them in hopes of building a partnership. I go about it backwards. I meet someone who might make a good partner and then get to know them in hopes of BECOMING attracted to them.

Without realizing it, David and I had been coming from opposite ends of the equation; our order of operations was reversed. David had simply been asking: Do you desire me?

Data Analysis:

We are far from alone in the endeavor to decipher the mysterious puzzle of human desire. The mad dash by pharmaceutical companies to crack the code to reignite waning lust is confirmation enough of the widespread (and profitable) interest in the subject. The question of female sexual desire in particular sparks feverish debate between 'Team Biology' and 'Team Psyche' over desire's place of origin. Are our desires birthed in our brains or bodies?

I suppose it took an overthinker's hubris to think I could plan my way into desire, but I knew I needed to crack it, that desire held a trove of useful information. It was apparent that those around me felt some qualitative difference between dating and friendship, but without a personal experience of sexual desire holding an intention, relationship building had always been just that. Spending time together, cultivating trust, revealing parts of self, increased care, becoming more comfortably and physically affectionate, this was how I did friendship. I did not have an alternate blueprint to build a relationship that might one day involve sex. And I hadn't been able to understand other people's distinction.

I can't guess, reader, whether you fall in the category of someone who knows exactly what I'm talking about or someone who can't fathom an existence without a sexual compass, but that morning standing in the kitchen I got it. I could sense the power of desire to clarify or confuse. I could see how picking a guy up at a bar or going on a match date could actually work for those who felt instant sexual stirrings upon meeting. Going on a first date would indeed be informative if you found yourself wanting the person sitting across the table. How wonderfully straightforward!

I turned a new eye to all of those perfectly pleasant first dates I'd been on years prior and the flat disinterest I'd felt for each and every one. I knew that I wasn't physically broken; if I could experience the physiology of desire in a dream, certainly it was possible in waking life. I was hungry to feel it again. I just had to figure out how.

Conclusion:

There are some things in this world that not even the most well laid plans nor well-kept calendars can control. Desire is one of these. When it comes to love, we can set our minds to polishing the dating profile, planning a date, rationally deciding who we marry, and meticulously controlling the wording of the pre-nup; but Desire, she will not take our direction. Our bodies are our desire Geiger counters, alerting us when she deigns to grace us with her presence, to the moment she has, on a whim, strolled through a room.

And I can tell you now, we need not fear her power as I once did. Though she is outside of our control, neither does she control us. She is our ally, our fellow researcher, delivering useful data, informing us of our reality. She points us towards what we want, holds our faces in front of it until we acknowledge that want, and in the acknowledgment, she relaxes. It's then up to us to choose how we move forward, how we integrate the new information she's gifted us. It's information no more frightening than *you're hungry* and no less urgent than *your hair is on fire.* "You want THIS."

We don't choose what we want, but we do choose whether and how we act once aware of the desire. Desire for our neighbor's wife will likely dictate different action than the desire for that piece of chocolate cake, but both feelings offer knowledge. Our desires tell us the story of what we want out of life, what type of person we want to be, what we find beautiful, and perhaps most importantly, what we feel is lacking in our lives. If we pay close enough attention to the story and follow the breadcrumbs of even the smallest desires, we can find ourselves on a path to the life we've always wanted.

Run Your Own Experiment No. 5:

The purpose of this experiment is to catalogue established desires so that we can methodically pursue or work around them when choosing to peruse relationship.

Experimental Procedure

1. On a piece of paper, write down ten traits your ideal partner would embody.

2. Once complete, consider your most significant romantic relationships. (If you have not yet been in a romantic relationship or would like a larger sample set, include those people you've felt drawn to be closer to and/or from whom you desire praise and attention.)

3. List the names of these people on a piece of paper.

4. Next to each name, write the traits they embody that you are attracted to. These traits may make logical sense to you or not; simply observe the facts and list them.

5. When complete, circle any items in these observations that also appear in the list from Step 1.

6. Now, review the observations that did not appear in Step 1. Are these traits you would like to add to that list? Are these traits you seem to be attracted to over and over again without being aware? Are these traits you would like to identify and avoid in future partners?

7. Thank Desire for all of this good information.

8. Hold on to these lists for a later experiment.

CHAPTER SIX
Establish Your Safety Protocol

safe·ty /ˈsāftē/:
the condition of being protected from undergoing or causing hurt, injury, or loss; the condition of being free from threat of harm or risk

SUBJECT: Overthinker; Female; Age 29 years, 11 months, 9 days.

HYPOTHESIS: There is a clear message within our culture that romance correlates with adventure and risk whereas routine, familiarity, and safety are romance killers. It follows, therefore, that my sleeping sexuality can be sparked only by what is dangerous and unknown.

METHOD: A friend, a horse wrangler, and a bisexual walk into a bar.

FIELD SITE: Tucked away in the back corner of a familiar small-town watering hole.

Experiment 140.22.8:

Kristen: Grab a beer?

Jonah: Sure. Can be there in 10.

As a rule, I didn't go out and drink when I was in the middle of a yoga workshop. I liked to hold the time sacred and let whatever was arising in meditation to process through me unaltered. But this felt like a beer conversation.

I hadn't breathed a word of my dream to anyone at the studio, not even my friend Naomi; it was too new, too enjoyably secret, too loaded. But by the end of the second day of meditation, I was itching to talk through it, and I knew exactly the sounding board I wanted sitting across from me.

I had a small crew I met most evenings at The Elk's Ear, a local biker bar turned quasi-family-friendly venue. Not quite as disciplined, vegetarian, or sober as my yogi crew, this cobbled together group of misfits satisfied within me a perfect counterpoint to the studio—another world view and language, a balance. I felt seen and heard by the whole group, but Jonah was the crew member I'd gotten closest to over the past seven months. We could talk about anything. He was familiar with my history of romantic bewilderment, and though he was in his mid 40s, he'd shared that he himself had only begun exploring shape of his own sexual orientation in recent years. I knew he would be a caring, accepting, and safe receiver of anything I could throw at him.

Feeling only slightly out of place in my uniform of stretchy pants and flowy wrap top, I grabbed a sticky table in a dimly lit spot at the back of the busy bar. I hadn't been there more than two minutes before Jonah walked in. I leapt out of my seat to greet him with a hug, and before our butts hit the seats, my mouth was off and running. It all came pouring out, David, the 'desire' mantra, the dream. Jonah listened with open interest, sipping the beer he'd managed to order us amidst my deluge of words. I came to the end of my report, taking my first real breath. "So, that's everything that's happened in just the last 48 hours. I don't know what any of it means yet."

He raised his glass in toast, "Well, that's exciting." I broke into a grin, feeling the charge, the buzz of nerves at acknowledging the now vast field of possible paths available to me. We clinked glasses, and he looked at me thoughtfully. "I know I've said this before, but you never cease to amaze me. You're constantly teaching me what it looks like to do the work and actually walk the walk. You've changed *so much* from the person I first met two years ago."

I bobbed my head in happy agreement, remembering back to the first time I'd met Jonah.

Jonah specialized in horse-based therapy and happened to be working with the kid of a cousin-by-marriage of mine when I came for a visit. He asked for my observations of the family structure. I recognized the feelings that come when someone is actually listening. I had newly begun therapy myself at the time and qualified Jonah's attentiveness as a characteristic of the line of work.

Over the next months I bumped into him a handful of times. In the brief back and forth we had in those moments I found myself telling him about difficulties with my job, my family, about the amazing like-souls I was meeting in my making-friends campaign around town, and even ended up sharing some of the more exciting self-revelations that were coming out of my therapy sessions. He knew some of my family, had an understanding of the therapeutic process, and, most importantly, he seemed genuinely interested. I, in turn, found myself effortlessly curious about what he had to say.

After a little more than a year, his work with my cousin had begun its natural tapering off, and we decided to purposely bump into one another for dinner one night. I'd driven to his place up the coast, and we walked from there to the restaurant where a friend of his was playing music. We talked more in depth than we had prior, and I continued to enjoy his company. But about thirty minutes in some part of me became concerned that he might be thinking we were on a date. Or that I thought it was a date. Or that it actually was a date. Or whether it even could be a date given that he was sixteen years older than I and had technically worked professionally with my family. I think the internal confusion began because I was drawn to be physically affectionate to Jonah the way I was drawn to be affectionate with all my friends—a bump of the shoulder, a hand on the arm, an appreciative hug—and for some reason the fact that he was male was throwing variables into the mental equation that left me uncertain of the solution. There was nothing apparently romantic going on, but I was a woman, and he was a man, and all of the alarms that reminded me that I was generally a bad read in these situations were going off, asserting that more likely than not I was doing it wrong.

He drove us home, and as we said goodnight my brain was like a computer misfiring, searching for the correct code for this encounter, still scanning the shelves for that missing gym-football playbook. *If I was out with a girlfriend, I'd hug her. If I hug him, is he going to try to kiss me? Do I want him to kiss me? Well, at least then it would be clear whether he thinks this is a date.* He didn't kiss me which was both a relief and left me still in the purgatory of wondering where his head was.

I got my answer about a week later when he returned from a trip. While sitting in my office at the insurance job, my cell buzzed.

Jonah: Can I call you?

Kristen: Yeah. Call my direct line.

I closed my office door just as the phone on my desk rang. "Hey! What's up?"

"Hey. Hi. I'm back in town, and I just really wanted to let you know that I've been doing a lot of soul searching this week while I was away, and I know I just need to do the right thing here. I of course find you attractive, and you have such a great soul—

My brain lagged behind my body in grasping what was occurring. It went physically rigid, flooded with embarrassed panic. I felt heat spike on my cheeks and held my breath, mortified, wanting to be anywhere but here holding this phone to my ear. The only saving grace was that he didn't seem to expect my participation in this monologue.

"—But I've come to the conclusion that I have to do the right thing here. I can't date you because I've worked with your family. I haven't taken this lightly. I *really* never expected to face this particular brand of ethical dilemma in my practice, and it isn't personal at all, and I'm really sorry if this is hurtful—"

His earnest soliloquy gave me time to drop out of my startled prey response and move towards recognition of and amusement in his boy-like discomfort.

"—It's just to protect everyone involved, including you. But I am totally comfortable with being friends if you're up for that. This all just took me by surprise, I didn't expect to ever have to deal with something like this."

By the time he finished my panic had passed. I spoke through a stifled smile, "Well. I'm glad I've been able to present you with a fresh and new dilemma, Jonah. I like to think I'm here in this life to help people stretch and grow however I can."

There was a beat, and then he began to laugh. Surprised, relieved of his script.

"*Of course* I understand, and no I don't take it personally. I'm flattered, actually. And yes, of course, I would very much like us to be friends. I genuinely enjoy our conversations."

The next time I saw him was a few days later while I was out with a girlfriend I affectionately referred to as Crazy Kat. She was the kind of hipster spiritual that could give you a contact high on all things woo-woo. Crystals and tarot and star charts and moon cycles. She seemed to have the boundless energy, intensity, and ever-hopping focus of a Chihuahua. I introduced Kat to Jonah, and when she heard what he did for a living she implored him to sit with us when he'd finished with his friends; it was a field of work she'd been looking to get into herself, and she wanted to pick his brain. That evening with Kat and Jonah marked the start of our little crew. We adopted a 30-something frustrated musician Jonah had befriended as our fourth, and before long we were nearly nightly fixtures at The Elk's Ear.

Those evenings of silliness and theorizing over beers became a lynchpin in my week, as important an element in my self-inquiry as my time spent in meditation. So, it was fitting, really, that I now sat mulling a meditation-catalyzed, mantra-dream revelation with my beer swilling, sexuality questioning, middle-aged, eternal bachelor, horse-wrangler friend. "I mean, I know that dreams rarely are literal—this one is, likely, what, an excitement to begin a relationship with my own femininity or a desirous wooing of some other previously neglected aspect of self or something."

"Yeah. Or maybe you just like girls."

I grinned. This was why I'd wanted Jonah here. The evening's direction launched into a playful, pseudo-discreet review of both the male and female patrons of the bar as he and I compared our taste in what we found attractive. As always, I could indicate those men and women I found to be aesthetically pleasing without any problem, but trying to wrap my brain around actually sleeping with one of them made me crinkle my nose like a 4-year-old faced with a plate of broccoli.

As we laughed my phone buzzed. An email from David flashed across the screen. I flicked the slider, my eyes skimmed until they landed on one line.

…It appears that you are indeed saying that you want to be just friends. I apologize, I believe that you made this point several times, it just took a little while to sink in…

"I think David got to it faster than I did."

"He text you?"

"Emailed." I put the phone down. "I realized yesterday morning that most people looking for a partner go in the order of: 1. Attraction, 2. Get to know them, 3. Hope they turn out to be solid partner material. I seem to go backwards. I choose people who seem like they'd make solid partners, get to know them, and then hope attraction arises." I leaned back in my chair, scrubbing my hands over my face in frustration. "And if I'm right, what does any of *this* matter?" waving my arms around widely, testing my balance in the chair, "Women, men, it's not like I needed a broader field—I mean, great, I could legitimately date a woman—but it still would mean I'd have to date! It's not like women are any easier. I mean, how do I even know if a woman is gay? Or not gay but open to a relationship? I mean, I don't even know if I am! It's so complicated! At least with men it's more obvious."

"You could go to a lesbian bar."

"Ha!" I let out a cynical laugh, "In LA? And date someone long distance? Ugh."

"You could go on tinder."

"In this small town? Pass." Jonah's look pointed me towards my fatalistic tone. "I'm sorry," I leaned forward in my chair, "It's just so daunting—*doubly* so now. I worked at trying to spark something with David, but if my reality is that I have to know someone before I become physically attracted to them, and even *then* maybe not, then these one-off meetings are just always going to be useless to me. I mean, I've always assumed I was going to get married and have lots of happy crazy sex with my husband and that it would all just come naturally. But I'm nearly thirty, and there's not a man or a woman I've ever come across and thought, 'I want to jump them.' Isn't that *weird*?"

"But you have been attracted to people."

"Sure. Not sexually though. I get attracted the way you get a friend crush on a new person you meet. You know, where you just want to be near them or touch them or spend time with them and have them like you. An emotional attraction, a meeting of like minds or souls or something."

"What about me? How early were you attracted to me?"

I'd never actually indicated I ever had been attracted in this way to Jonah. But I had. "Early" I nodded, "Honestly, I figured it was just because I was enamored with all things therapy at the time." I grinned at him and nodded at my beer, "I never guessed we'd end up drinking buddies!"

"Do you remember when that was? When you first felt that? Because I think I can tell you right when it was."

"Oh, gosh," I looked to the ceiling, thinking. "Probably when we were at my cousin's house—"

"Way back then!?" He was surprised.

"Yeah, when we first sat down and talked one on one in those family interviews you did."

"See, I would have said when I was with your family at your place."

"That Thanksgiving?"

"Yeah, I could feel—is it okay that we're talking about this, by the way?"

I waved off the question, "Of course! How else are we going to analyze the data?"

"Right. Yeah, I could see you were controlling it."

I looked at him dubiously, "Of course, then there was the night we went out, and I didn't know if it was a date —"

"Yeah, me neither.

"You didn't!?"

"I didn't think it was, but then about half way through, I thought, 'Whoa, this is feeling a lot like a date,' and I started doing the math in my head wondering, 'Can I do this?'"

I was incredulous. "You were doing the math *while* we were out!?"

"Yeah. It had only been six months since I'd last worked with your cousin." The generally accepted ethic was that at least twenty-four months were supposed to pass between end of treatment and any social contact between therapist and client. Of course, I wasn't one of his clients. I was the second cousin once removed by marriage of one of his clients.

"Oh my gosh." I shook my head, laughing. "Well, I just assumed it couldn't possibly be a date. Though there was the tiniest flash of wondering when we got back home and said our goodnights. I thought you might try to kiss me or something."

The conversation was so easy, so un-awkward, just two friends examining what amounted to yet another case study from my past in the grand cause of helping me pinpoint what it was that might lead to my next relationship frontier. When I left the bar that night I felt light and happy and excited to have someone solidly in support of wherever I was going to search for romance. In those few hours Jonah and I had dropped even more deeply into the relaxed freedom of our friendship. The kind available to two people between whom nothing is unspoken.

At home I let my thoughts wander as I brushed my teeth, recapping the evening. My hand froze, mid-brush, and my gaze snapped to meet my own eyes in the mirror. Out of the blue I suddenly knew, very soon, I was going to find myself kissing Jonah.

Data Analysis:

Chastity came easy for me. Anyone who's grown up in the church knows that the mandate of remaining a virgin until marriage is a struggle for many if not most, but for me 'because God said so' was a handy short-hand explanation for my natural inclinations. The knowledge of my virginity was like a little box tied to my belt that was just always bopping along behind me, solid, dependable, true. I didn't think of it often. It had become the tchotchke on the mantel that you know is there but no longer register as your eyes pass over it. Until one day something in the back of your brain starts to itch, alerting you to the fact that something is different. The itch wakes you up, makes you properly look again, only to discover that the reliable little nick-knack is missing. That item you'd taken for granted is suddenly quite a compelling mystery.

Once struck with the knowing that I was about to find myself in some sort of physical relations with Jonah, I reflexively whipped around to consult my life-long companion of chastity. My backwards glance revealed a tether flapping in the wind, no longer tied to anything. This development was, to say the least, curious. I checked again the next day to see if perhaps it was a temporary anomaly, but still, there was only empty space where the tidy box of identity had once been. So, like any sane, normal human being, I went for a hike and struck up an inquiry with the voices in my head.

Alright, this is weird. Why would a three-decade-old tenant of self just up and disappear?

Let's see if we can trace this step by step. What did my little box provide me?

The knowledge we were safe.

Wow, you had that answer cued right up, didn't you?

Yep.

At its core, our chastity has kept us safe from a lot of things, hasn't it? Emotional entanglement, feeling beholden, the limitations of a relationship, pregnancy, STDs, marriage, insanity—I could go on...

You know I'm right.

I can see you're right.

Okay, so if we apparently no longer need our chastity to keep us safe, we must be getting our safety fix somewhere else. But where?

What's providing us with a sense of safety now?

Together, my inner analysts broadened our attention to survey the field of my life at that moment. Scenes and feelings flooded through: the deep belonging that washed over me each time I crossed the threshold of the yoga studio, the love poured into me by the incredible women there, the laughter and intimate sharing of my morning walks with Naomi, the encouragement I received to explore every wild possibility for my life via the enthusiastic cheerleading of my Elk's Ear crew, the open understanding I'd found in Jonah, my friend and advocate, the pure magic that permeated this life I inhabited, doing nothing I was 'supposed' to do and yet somehow getting away with it, feeling full and joyful and valued, and resting in the sense that I was being taken care of by something bigger than myself.

This life. Look at everything I've been blessed with. God doesn't want me to come to harm. God's got me. Given me all this. These amazing people in my life love me, hold me, make me feel safe.

I felt safe, so the old boogeymen had lost their bite, and a new world of possibilities had opened up before me.

Conclusion:

I know I'm not alone in having nearly reached thirty without ever having had a sexual encounter. Just recently I heard a piece on NPR's "Morning Edition" noting that, "A series of studies have come out in one of the leading sex research journals finding that people are having sex less frequently, that young adults—people in their twenties—are more likely to have been celibate in adulthood and that they are on track to have fewer lifetime sexual partners than either Boomers or Gen Xers have had." Scientists appear to still be parsing out the cause of this shift, but one theory is that people coming of age in this era may struggle with intimacy in this world of swipe-right.

So, let us turn our attention to the jungles and desert plains, to our wild cousin creatures of the swamps and those hidden deep in the forests. When threat and danger arise, there is a biological response in all animals (including humans) that you have likely heard of before: it is the fight, flight, freeze or fold response. The amygdala sets off an alarm, throwing the body into a survival state. Optimistic bodily functions like digestion, elimination, and procreation immediately shut down. Our human bodies react to 'benign' stress in the exact same way they would respond to a jaguar ready to pounce, leaving many of us chronically in this state of the 4Fs. (It's no surprise, then, that stress is such a leading cause of illness in our modern culture.) Biological safety is the absence of the 4Fs. And safety is essential for physical intimacy.

Alright, alright, calm down, I'm not advocating boring sex here. It's entirely possible for some of the most poignant emotional safety to be present amidst the most raucous, acrobatic, death-defying and potentially illegal sex acts of which two people are capable. Because safety means something different to everyone. In fact, it means something different to a single human being based on their past experiences, stage of life, context of the moment, and whether he or she woke up this morning feeling sexy or bloated.

For my thirty-one-year-old divorced girlfriend, safety is no-strings-attached sex.

For another, it is being with someone completely unavailable.

For many of the people I grew up with, safety is the commitment of marriage.

For some it is total anonymity.

For one adventuresome gal I know, it's the word 'porcupine.'

For still others, safety is friendship and well-established trust.

Just as safety can look different for different people, it also comes in different degrees. We each have a threshold we cross to move into the territory of 'safe enough.' That transition occurs at a different point depending on our innate tolerance for risk. Just as some of us have a taste for jumping out of airplanes while others find trying out a new hairstyle to be daring enough, some of us simply require more or less holding than others to feel safe. And likewise, you may feel more daring in a given moment, your safety/risk bar temporarily shifted, because you did, indeed, happen to wake up on the sexy side of the bed today. It's up to each of us to establish what feels safe to us, seek that, communicate it to our partners, and update them when it changes.

When it comes down to it, each of these apparently incongruous definitions of safety all point towards the same thing. Feeling safe allows us to feel free. Free to show up as ourselves, as we choose to be. Free to trust. Free to let go. Okay, now that sounds sexy.

Run Your Own Experiment No. 6:

The purpose of this experiment is to identify our current zones of safety so that we can intentionally craft more of them within future and existing relationships.

Experimental Procedure

1. Retrieve your list from Experiment No. 2. That is, the thoughts, behaviors, or emotions you've masked in past relationships.

2. Consider whether there have been any relationships— romantic or not, personal, professional, or therapeutic—in which you have talked about or shown these parts of self. Write down the names of those who come to mind.

3. What circumstances were specifically present in each relationship that allowed you to feel safe enough to introduce these parts of yourself? Write these down.

4. Once complete, read through your answers and circle the qualities or phrases that you would like to be present in all of your relationships, specifically your romantic ones.

Bonus Steps

1. As you go into the world today and interact with the people in your life, hold these qualities in mind and ask yourself which ones each person you interact embodies. Consider whether you would feel safe sharing parts of yourself with them.

2. If the answer is 'No,' consider these questions:

   a. How does the relationship serve me as it stands currently? What am I getting out of it?

   b. What would be the real-world consequences to me showing up as I choose to within this relationship?

3. Weighing these answers, make a conscious decision to either:

   a. Continue the relationship as it is in order to reap what it provides you.

   b. Experiment by showing up as you would like to and confirm whether your hypothesis of consequences was correct.

CHAPTER SEVEN

Allow for Knowledge in Advance of Evidence

ev·i·dence /ˈevədəns/:
the available body of facts or information indicating
whether a belief or proposition is true or valid;
ground for belief; proof

SUBJECT: Overthinker; Female; Age 29 years 11 months, 25 days.

HYPOTHESIS: Knowledge and understanding come by hard data and supporting proof. In the quest to understand my world this is the only type of knowledge I can trust.

METHOD: Confidants, clairvoyance, copulation.

FIELD SITE: A quintessential one-room, Ikea-furnished, converted-garage-apartment bachelor pad.

Experiment 140.40.3:

I knew I was about to find myself in a physical relationship with Jonah, and I had no idea why. I didn't want to marry him. I didn't even want to date him. No way I wanted to bring him home to my parents. I could look at him with a discerning eye and know that he was pretty good looking for a man of forty-six, but I wasn't even yet thirty; there were many younger, fitter, empirically more attractive men out there who would happily fool around with me.

There had been no indication in the past couple months of our deepening friendship that either of us had designs on moving things in a physical direction. And yet, here we were. I was so fascinated by this unshakable internal certainty of the future that I had to tell someone. I needed to hear it aloud, look at it, roll it around to make sure it felt real.

Naomi, my closest confidant and yoga instructor, blinked wide as I shared the news while we were on our daily hike the next morning. "Wow."

"I know. I don't really know how to explain it. It's like it's already happened. Like the present time is simply catching up with what's already in the past. It's like I've pulled my head up and read the direction of the river I was already riding. I can see where it's heading."

She knew exactly what I was talking about. This was why we were friends.

That evening, sitting under the stars drinking beer with my small crew at The Elk's Ear, Jonah announced that he was moving away. He'd leave town in two months. I was stunned. Not only because the news came with no warning, but because it seemed our impending dalliance had just gotten a whole heck of a lot less complicated. There was now a nice, neat expiration date. I was quickly becoming convinced of this persistent knowing and settled more deeply into the sense of being held by some master plan at work. I made a mental note that perhaps I should bring it up with Carla on our phone call that evening.

If I haven't mentioned it before, I should mention it now, I live in a funky little town in Southern California where even the most straight-laced resident has a little woo-woo in them. I'm originally from the Midwest where your doctor is the GP you've been seeing since you were born and physical therapy is considered alternative medicine. Out here, though, everyone has a Chinese medicine trained acupuncturist, an Ayurvedic healer, and cranio-sacral specialist who dabbles in myofascial release on the side. It's a place where the phrase "Mercury is in retrograde" is met with solemn nods, and people argue the finer points of Western versus Vedic astrological chart readings, gasping if they discover you don't know the house in which your moon falls. (I never have been able to remember).

After living here a handful of years, I consider myself to be what you might call woo-adjacent. I have always been a church-going gal of faith, and I've never felt any conflict between my religion, yogic texts, psychotherapy and woo-woo—to me it all sounds like the same lessons being shared in different languages. So, while at that time I didn't necessarily go so far as to claim that I 'believed' I'd had past lives or that the flip of a card could declare my future nor the stars my past, I also couldn't say that any of it made me uneasy. In fact, I'd come to find much of the woo quite useful. Nothing else I'd ever encountered had been able to so efficiently combat my overthinking and reveal what I really wanted than the millisecond pause that came *after* asking a question and *before* receiving an answer from the consulted. It was a crystalized moment of pure, raw, naked clarity.

So, it was only a minor stretch that after I'd had my dream of desire I scheduled a phone session with Naomi's favorite Jungian analyst turned full time intuit, Carla. The fact that Carla was a nice, respectable retiree who had practiced accredited Western mainstream methods before transitioning to full on woo-woo made her approachable in my mind. In perfect timing, Jonah had made the announcement of his impending departure just hours before our scheduled call. I prepared my space before sitting down to dial her number. A comfortable but supportive chair pulled up to my kitchen table, a full glass of water, the lighting set just so, pen, paper, recorder, a brand new unopened deck of playing cards, and the page of questions I'd written out in preparation.

I sat down and watched the clock tick down the last two minutes doing internal inventory. I expected to feel nervous or anxious or spooky—I'd never taken part in anything this un-Midwestern—but instead, I was pleasantly surprised to find myself in calm anticipation as though I was about to have a friendly chat with God. That made me laugh. *Who knows? God works in mysterious ways.*

Carla was lovely, her voice that of a woman in her seventies but her energy seemingly boundless. She began by explaining her methods, "I use playing cards because they're a universal language, and I have you pull them because it's *your* unconscious speaking. I'll also be consulting your guides." Carla's description of my "guides" was something akin to guardian angels—beings in some non-earthly realm who were karmically assigned to me or took a personal interest in my life. Angels were a normal part of my Christian background, and I didn't hate the idea that there might be a few of them floating around with vested interests in my well-being.

"Alright then, let's just ease in by getting a kind of overall message for you, alright?"

"Okay, great." She instructed me to shuffle and then cut the cards as many times as felt correct before fanning them out on the table in front of me. I pulled six cards out of the spread and turned them over one by one.

"Four of hearts." Carla tells me this indicates pure love, innocence, and new opportunities to gather learnings I missed as a child.

"Seven of clubs." New opportunities are opening for me.

"Seven of hearts." Wishes being fulfilled. It's a promise card. What's required is for me to decide now what my shifting wishes actually are.

"Jack of clubs." An advice card. Proceed step by step.

"Another seven! You know, that's my lucky number. My birthdate.

This time it's of diamonds." I'm moving into a new flourishing of body, desires, connectivity, and partnership. I will be in deep relationship that leaves me feeling more than I was, expanded, and I'm being sent more than one person so I can better know who I am.

"Jack of spades." One of the partners being sent my way will stoke the fire of interest in the world and my taste for adventure. They won't be the one but will be a great energizer and make me different.

"Alright, that's a great place to start, so let's turn to some of your specific questions now."

The session found a rhythm, me pulling cards, Carla explaining their meaning to me with the help of my guides and dousing them with the occasional bit of Jungian flair. We covered it all, from career, "What is my work in the world?"

Ten of spades, ten of clubs, eight of clubs.

"Teaching. Or counseling. Your guides don't want you wasted on individuals though. If you set up your own office you'd get irritated because you'd end up with a bunch of self-centered men making a mess of things. Groups. A big soul needs a big canvas. Keep your eyes peeled for opportunities to create a course. You're going to be teaching all your life—you already have been."

To going back to school: king of hearts, two of clubs, six of spades.

"You won't learn much you don't already know, but that 'official standing' of a title or endorsement would feel good to you. It might solve your insecurity and low self-esteem in the eyes of others."

To uncertain friendships: six of diamonds, five of spades, eight of spades; then nine of spades, queen of diamonds

"She's afraid of disappointing you, and even though it's unfounded, you're going to have to let her go and come back. You have a unique capacity to shift and switch between relationship dynamics. Most people can't do that so easily. It's a real gift. She can't shift that quickly, but she will come back."

And money: five of hearts

"You'll have money, but it's going to come to you in unusual ways. It's not going to be a salary."

After seventy-five minutes we adopted the socially dictated sounds and tones to indicate that we both knew the call was coming to an end, but just as I was about to sign off, I blurted out, "Oh, wait! I'm so sorry, I know we're over time, but I have one more question, and if I don't ask it I just know I'll regret it forever."

Carla responded with spunky curiosity, "Well then, you better ask it!"

"Okay! Thank you. Yes. There's a friend of mine, and I have the sense that I'm going to be in a physical relationship with him. And I just want to know whether that would be a great thing or if it would be a terrible idea."

"Well, let's find out. Pull three cards." There were few cards left, maybe a third of the deck, so I was able to shuffle and spread them more easily now. One, two, three, I slid each card out without too much thought, turned each one over, and relayed their suits and numbers. Carla was quiet, so I waited in breathless silence for one beat...two beats...

A surprised peal of laughter broke through from the other end of the line. "Well, *that* was not the answer I was expecting!" She continued jovially, "For one thing, I have to start with this: your guides over here," I imagined her gesturing to the cosmos above her head, "are cheering you on telling you to go for it. They all seem to think it's a fabulous idea. And then these *cards*! Well, the four of spades is telling you to stop worrying so much. You don't need to spin out all of the possible outcomes. You're overthinking this for nothing. The second one, the ace of hearts, is the Self card. It's telling us that this experience will be all about you and *your* journey. Your discovery of yourself for yourself. And the six of clubs—well, this is the absolute sexiest card in the entire deck! Listen, you're not going to fall in love with this guy, but you're going to learn a lot.

She continued, "This really is a surprise. When you asked this question, I expected you to get a big fat 'no,' and let me tell you why.

You've been pulling from the same deck all evening, and I know *exactly* which cards are left in the stack in front of you. Nearly every one of them is a seriously thorny card. The odds of you pulling these three—" I could practically hear her shaking her head through the telephone, "—well, you certainly got a clear answer! This friend is there as a provider of an experience for you. Supportive, solid, only there for your good, to allow you to connect with yourself in a precious way."

I thanked her profusely for the extra time, she wouldn't let me pay her anything more, and hung up the phone. I can't say for certain whether everything that followed would have happened differently if I'd pulled the death and destruction card with Carla, but I didn't. It appeared all systems were go. I slumped back into my chair, looked up at the ceiling, and scrubbed my hands over my face. I let out a guffaw. "I guess this is what's happening."

I made it to my thirtieth birthday. My virginity did not.

It began with me informing Jonah a few days after my session with Carla, "You know we're going to have a physical relationship before you leave."

"We are?"

"Yeah. And it seems my guides are all for it." We made out on his bed a few minutes later.

A couple of days after that we made out again, this time unencumbered by clothing. In the midst of things, Jonah paused, peered down at my face, and earnestly assured me, "I know your decision to not have sex before marriage is really important to you."

The third time, when he looked at me with a questioning glint in his eye, I shrugged assent.

"Are you sure?"

I found it anti-climactic that this moment didn't feel like some big life-changing decision. Instead, it felt as though his question held all the weight of a waitress asking me whether I wanted fries or a side salad. I was an adult. I trusted Jonah. I felt safe with him.

He was dear to me. He knew me, knew my history or lack thereof. He would be careful with me, guide me, take care of me. I nodded, "Yeah." He got a condom.

I've always hated the phrase, 'lost my virginity.' It felt more like I 'let go' of my virginity that day. And I didn't 'give' it to anyone either. I simply released it like relaxing my hold on the string of a balloon. This re-categorization that had once in theory seemed so ponderous and life-changing felt, in act, like a mere matter of semantics. Penis .0001 mm from hymen. Virgin. A negligible movement. Penis .0001 mm past hymen. Not virgin. A core cultural definition of a human determined within a matter of millimeters.

I actually wasn't even totally certain when the switch officially occurred. The big moment just felt like a sort of indistinguishable pressure down there. I mean, I knew when it hadn't happened yet, and then I knew when we were officially having the sex, but I couldn't feel for myself that moment of transition. It was almost funny to think that the only person on the planet who might have actually experienced the instant of my state change wasn't even me, it was the person on top of me. But experienced or not, in that fraction of a second, my present caught back up to what I'd been feeling had somehow already occurred in the past. I still didn't know how we'd gotten here, but I felt relaxed that everything was happening exactly as it should.

Data Analysis:

In 1915 Einstein introduced his general theory of relativity, and with it, rewrote the rules of space and time. It was here he asserted that disturbances in the cosmos quite literally compressed space-time in one direction while stretching it in the other, a phenomenon that produced what he called gravitational waves.

Now, back then there existed no equipment sensitive enough to even begin to detect these waves, yet amazingly, few in the scientific community doubted that they were real. In fact, there was such strong belief in this unprovable theory that hundreds of millions of dollars were committed to build the Laser Interferometer Gravitational-Wave Observatory (LIGO), a facility whose *sole* purpose was to measure this possibly nonexistent and probably immeasurable wave. In 2017, over a hundred years after Einstein first shared his discovery of gravitational waves with the world, a team of scientists detected the collision of two black holes in a far corner of our universe and were able to measure, in a fraction of a second, the resultant gravitational wave. Knowledge we'd held for over a century had finally been united with its evidence.

We've all experienced moments when we've acted out of some indefensible certainty. I wondered whether it would take me as long as Einstein to understand why I'd let go of my virginity seemingly out of the blue. Over the course of six weeks Jonah and I slept together a handful of times. Sex became a shared pastime, a new option to add to the list of evening activities: grab a beer with the crew, see a movie, or go have sex. And it was nice. I mean, the being close part was, the expanded language of intimacy that sex afforded. I discovered that, because the sex had been had, I'd gained access to a previously unknown interstitial zone of physical activities. Simply because sex was now on the table, I was now allowed to engage in normal non-sexual friend activities while wearing fewer clothes, with more freedom of affectionate touch, fewer boundaries, and more skin-to-skin restfulness. It was as though I'd stumbled upon the secret password to a members-only club. I was privy to an entire landscape of pre and post-sex physical intimacy, the kind of physical intimacy I'd always craved without knowing it existed. Sex itself didn't do much for me, but this, *intimacy...this is what I want!*

It wasn't as though sex itself was bad or uncomfortable. In a lot of ways I felt the same way I had kissing Phillip or making out with David; I didn't hate it, but it didn't do much for me. It was a blip on the radar in what I now understood to be the grand scheme of physical intimacy. The most ominous aspects of sex's reputation—the hook of the hormones, the physical hunger for the pleasure—true to pattern, just never showed up for me. True, I felt as much love for my friend I ever had, but no unbidden visions of white picket fences or urges to bear his children reared their forceful heads. Sex inspired neither hunger nor madness nor poetry in me.

But the tweener zone did. Now that I'd experienced this secret interstitial space first hand, it seemed so silly that we weren't all taking advantage of this magical realm with everyone. This physical language of intimacy, closeness, love, and trust that spoke volumes of deep connection where words alone faltered felt useful regardless of the categorical definition of the relationship. To me, this language of intimacy felt totally separate from sex.

But therein laid the problem. Others seemed to connect these two landscapes. Would I only ever gain access to this place if I was willing to have sex with the other person? Could it really be that this realm of expression is only available to us if we come to accept intercourse as the endgame? And even if I was willing to accept such a toll, what of the dear relationships in which sex wasn't an option? It seemed impossibly unfair. That as girlfriends we aren't allowed to cozy up on the couch in our underwear and watch a movie, or that we're not supposed to spoon skin to skin under a blanket to nap together with a sweet friend or get to share a bath with graceful ease and joy at being close, open, truly in the vulnerable reality of one another's existence. I may not have understood why I'd had sex, but doing so gave me a peek into the deep, layered intimacy this category of human relationship might have to offer me. How was I going to return to a land of such restrictive and limited expression of relationship? How would I find others like me out there in the world? And, what if there weren't any?

Conclusion:

Sometimes we know what's happening before we know why it's happening. More often than not we overthinkers write that knowing off as wishful thinking or a runaway imagination. But particularly in the realm of relationship, in our interactions with other human beings, it behooves us to think twice before brushing off our pre-evidence-understanding.

It can be unnerving or even frightening to those of us seeking an existence of cool-headed logic to think that we might find ourselves with knowledge of a situation we can't support. In fact, it is not unusual to simply shut those inklings down out of that very fear. We chastise ourselves for getting a creepy vibe from that guy on the bus who is probably perfectly nice. We second guess the lightning-sharp certainty we have that our partner is cheating, recasting our knowledge as unfounded (and unflattering) jealousy. We allow self-doubt to dampen the little voice trying to get our attention to tell us that pretty girl didn't just accidentally lean her arm against ours, *she actually likes us!* and miss the opportunity to strike up a relationship. But we need not fear these moments of apparently unfounded knowledge for they are actually science at work!

One sunny afternoon, my friend found his bike inexplicably veering off a path, crashing into the brush and scraping himself up royally. Baffled, it wasn't until he stood up and brushed himself off that he saw the tail of a massive rattle snake slithering through the path. In that moment, he was grateful, as we all would be, that his body had perceived what his conscious brain had not. Had he waited to fully understand the situation, it would have been too late! Our physical bodies evolved over millennia to read with incredible accuracy where we stand in relationship to the world around us. It is her job to shorthand that which would take far too long to consciously explain, to flood our systems with a sense of dread, longing, excitement, fear, and curiosity as appropriate to inspire us to flee from the stalking predator, find the nearest food source, and prime us to shore up our safety through tribal bonds.

Our radar is constantly picking up and assimilating unconscious cues being unknowingly broadcast by those around us, and often the conclusions that bubble up from this unseen data analysis can be interpreted as unfounded guesswork by our rational brains. To accept them as genuine knowledge requires trust. If we are to benefit from knowing what we know more quickly, our brains must have faith that they are working in concert with our entire system and that there is wisdom to be found outside of that which we can break down and language into if/then proofs. We overthinkers can find solace in the reframe that it would simply be *illogical* to not make use of every tool available to our learning.

It's hard to believe what we can't prove. Even Einstein wavered. He knew gravitational waves were real, but without being able to point to hard evidence in the physical world, he twice lost faith and attempted to debunk his own theory before flip flopping back again. Self-trust isn't easy, it takes practice. But it's also worth it. I can't help but wonder what other incredible truths Einstein might have discovered had he not wasted that time attempting to un-know that of which he was already certain.

Run Your Own Experiment No. 7:

The purpose of this experiment is to discover how much we already know so that we may expand our understanding and enroll this skill in the task of building & guiding new relationships.

It can be easier to tap into this sense of non-evidenced knowing when focusing on warning signals, perhaps because our biology has developed to allow those to ring more loudly in order to focus us on a life or death threat. It is for this reason we focus on this type of knowledge in the following experiment.

Experimental Procedure

1. Consider an incident in which you've uttered the words akin to, "I should have known," "I always had a funny feeling about," "I missed all the warning signs," after the end of a relationship. If a romantic partnership doesn't come to mind, choose another type of relationship for this experiment.

2. At the top of your paper write this person's name.

3. Beneath that, write about your experience of this person prior to the incident.

4. Now consider the state of things after the incident. List any behaviors you witnessed but missed warning signs as well as the ways you wrote off or explained those behaviors at the time.

5. Knowing what you know now, knowing your feelings were spot on, write an answer to these questions: Why didn't you act then? Would you do anything differently?

Bonus Steps

1. Close your eyes and drop into the physical feeling you had when you were writing off those missed warning signs.

2. Holding that feeling, consider whether there are any current relationships in which you carry a similar sense that you are waving away a deeper knowing.

PART II:

Unanticipated Experimental Results

CHAPTER EIGHT
Love Follows the Law of Conservation of Energy

law of conservation of energy:
the total energy of an isolated system remains
constant; energy can neither be created nor
destroyed; rather it can only be transformed from
one form to another

SUBJECT: Overthinker; Female; Age 30 years, 2 months, 4 days.

HYPOTHESIS: My love is generated through external circumstances. When I am surrounded by those I love I get to feel loving towards them, and when they are removed, my ability to generate love disappears with them.

METHOD: Emotional good-byes, malfunctioning hGC detectors, a Tibetan Buddhist nun.

FIELD SITE: Long stretches of US interstate carrying me from home to acceptance.

Experiment 140.062.9:

By chance or design, Crazy Kat unexpectedly got a job out of state that had her moving out of town within hours of Jonah's departure. For two weeks before they left grief resonated through my bones. I'd experienced lows before, but this one claimed my physical self in a way that was new. I told Naomi on one of our walks that I felt like I was in the shadow of an impending death. I cried. When I was too dehydrated to cry I stared unseeing at the television until a sad or tender or completely innocuous commercial came on, and then I'd cry some more. I was too exhausted to get off the couch, lead limbs landing where they would and staying there for hours.

I grieved the end of this charmed little circle of safety and support that had given me a sense of acceptance unlike any I'd experienced. This perfect equation of time and place and people was evaporating; the magic, fairy-dust-sprinkled spring of slow, warm evenings filled with boisterous laughter and relaxed silences, confessions and explorations, earnest questioning and silliness unspoken over the rim of a cold beer and the lilt of a vaguely country-flavored tune floating over the patio, already these things had become artifacts belonging to a past season. I felt like a high school senior in my last summer and mourned the death of a time to which I knew I'd never be allowed to return.

My friends drove off in the wee hours of the morning. The final nail in the coffin was delivered, and though I'd never looked more like a hysterical woman than that day, the echo of the hammer also held the promise of relief. You see, there, just beneath the dying, I had been sensing a beginning. It had been my experience that birth and death were two sides of the same coin. Each required the other. Every time a part of my life had ended, a day would come where I could look back and say, because of that end, I was allowed this miraculous beginning. Finally, with the end complete, I felt I could look forward to that new life.

And I already believed it would be the start of something

wonderful. Just ten days after The Elk's Ear crew disbanded, I was scheduled to leave on a two-week road trip with Naomi to sit in practice with a Tibetan Buddhist nun visiting the mountains of Wyoming. The plan was to road trip though the national parks and take in terrain and vistas like none I'd ever seen. Naomi had invited me to join her six months earlier when our friendship had still been in its infancy. Sitting in meditation with a nun had felt completely above my novice yogi paygrade, yet I'd said yes. Now I marveled at the elegant timing. This adventure would launch me into whatever was coming next, the new creative project I sensed welling up within me, preparing itself to be birthed into the world. I was excited to move through the last of the grief and into a phase of energy and building. For surely, this phase of death was now complete.

My grandmother called me at 9:30 AM two days after my friends had moved away. "Kristen? This is Bagga. Your granddad—"

The moment I registered her tone I cut her off, "I'm hanging up and calling an ambulance."

"Oh, he doesn't want that... Chuck?... Should we call an ambulance?...Chuck?"

"I'm coming up RIGHT NOW, and I am CALLING AN AMBULANCE." I hung up the phone and dialed 911 with one hand and pulled clothes on with the other.

"This is 911, please state the nature of your emergency."

"My name is Kristen Smith. My address is 2782 East Avenue. I need an ambulance. There is something wrong with my grandfather." I was sprinting the hundred yards from my place to theirs.

"Alright, Ma'am. Can you tell me what's happening? What are his symptoms?"

"He has COPD." I burst through the front door of my grandparents' place making a beeline to the bedroom. My granddad was sitting half upright on the edge of the bed. My mostly-blind grandmother hovered next to him repeating his name over and over. Though his back was to me, I had a clear view of his face in the mirror. "He's vomited. It looks like it might be a stroke. One side of his face looks like it's fallen. He can't seem to sit upright."

"There's an ambulance on the way. Is he conscious?"

"His eyes are open. You need to tell the ambulance that we're the second house, not the one on the street. They have to drive back into the orchard." Granddad made an incoherent sound, a cross between a moan and an attempt to form words.

"Was that him?" The operator had overheard the noise, "Can he speak?"

"No. I think he's trying to, but it's not words."

The paramedics walked directly through the front door and into the bedroom as though my grandfather had been fitted with a homing beacon. I stepped out of their way and into the kitchen. A woman began asking me questions. I gave her the full rundown of Granddad's medical history.

About a year after I'd moved into the little guesthouse on my grandparents' orchard, my granddad had started getting sick. They said it was COPD which essentially meant that his lungs were doing a crap job of getting oxygen to his body. I come from a breed of people whose cure for a common cold is to go out to the field and pull a plow for 8 hours, whose remedy for a broken bone is to simply refuse to accept that it's broken. This past year had been an uncomfortable landscape for everyone, an endless stream of doctors' visits and insurance paperwork for oxygen tanks and masks and pumps, convincing him to do what the doctor told him to do, and convincing my grandmother that no, making him walk laps around the house and turning the oxygen pump down to two instead of ten would not, in fact, make his lungs stronger. It would, in fact, kill him.

I'd been preparing for this moment on some level for a while, listening to his nurses and tracking his diagnosis more intently as of late. I realized as I watched the paramedics wheel him out to the ambulance that I'd been secretly hoping to get a frantic call from my grandmother one morning saying he wouldn't wake up. I know he'd have preferred dying in his sleep to whatever was about to occur.

By now the neighbors had joined us in the front yard and were sharing supportive words. I had my grandmother pack a few things and called my parents in Chicago, my sister in San Francisco, my brother in New York. Then I called my uncle to meet us. Upon arrival I discovered that hospitals were not my uncle's strong suit. I found him down the hall staring at the faux-art screwed into the hallway wall. The few times he spoke to the doctors his information about Granddad was so wrong or outdated that I had to keep interjecting. The nurses began to turn to me as their point person.

When they finally took us back to see Granddad in his hospital bed, I stepped out immediately to call my mom. "You should book the first flight out." Granddad was in the hospital for three days before they called to say he was near the end. Our family met for breakfast that morning at a country kitchen near the hospital. We joked that it was the generations of Tennessee plantation work in our history that made us turn to biscuits in times of grief. We swapped stories about Granddad around the table and continued once we'd relocated to his bedside. For an hour we talked over, around, and to his silent body.

"Do you remember that time he got so mad at Bobby that he came tearing out of the front door in his underwear chasing him? He was half way down the street before he realized!"

"Or how much he loved giving those hayrides to all the grandkids? I never saw him so happy as when he would pull that tractor around and drive us all back for s'mores."

"And how proud he was of all of those dirty signs he had nailed up in the old barn? He had to take half of them down when we had the family reunion out here."

"And he loved you grandkids so much. I couldn't believe how much he softened when you came along, Kristen."

"He even stopped smoking and cursing!"

"He kept one vice, though. I was twenty before I realized his water glass was full of vodka!"

"Well, you can take the bartender out of Chicago…"

In moments of lull, we sang hymns, unbothered by how our untrained voices clunked against one another in the small room.

"Remember when we were living on Oak Street, and—"

"Mom, I think he stopped breathing."

The room fell silent, all eyes riveted on the pale blue hospital blanket tucked around the frail bones of this once barrel-chested man. For one second...two seconds...five seconds...a breath! We swarmed the bed, everyone placing a hand on him, grasping his fingers, his arms, his feet. We prayed aloud. Tears streaming, we inelegantly thanked God for him, for the gift of his life, for the gift of having him in our lives. We were all there in a room with a man we loved. And then, in the span of a single breath not taken, we were in a room with a body. We cried. We sang. We prayed. And then we planned.

Everyone ended up at my grandparents' place, everyone on a cell phone handling a different moving part—my father with the pastor, my mother with the caterers, my sister with flowers while I began culling through photos for the slideshow. My family's breed is also the type that does well in crisis. We were like a well-oiled machine. I thought at one point, no one should be this good at pulling together a funeral.

Friends from Houston texted that they'd seen the facebook post of Granddad's passing, and were we hungry? By the time the food they ordered for us was delivered the entire funeral had been planned. My mother had wanted the service to be on Sunday, the day I was to leave for Wyoming. I breathed a sigh of relief to find the pastor was only available Saturday. I would be able to attend.

The burial was a private affair, just immediate family. I had felt an extra pang of sorrow at realizing I 'knew the routine.' Granddad was the third grandparent I'd watched lowered into his final resting place in three short years. The few forlorn folding chairs propped up in the midst of the cemetery telegraphing the location of the plot, the faux golf course green grass draped between the casket and the lawn obscuring the view of the hole that had been dug beneath, the basket full of the flowers we would each place in turn on top of the shiny wood that housed his body. These elements had become familiar. The whole ritual was brief and dignified. Then back into the cars to the memorial service.

The church was packed out. It struck me as we walked in greeted by the multimedia slide show, that funerals and weddings—both of which seemed abundant at this stage of my life—were strangely similar. Music, speeches meant to make us laugh and cry, a neatly packaged and presented story of a life, the awkwardness of a minister who may have met the family once or twice, the programs, the focus on their more admirable qualities and good-natured poking at the faults, the flowers, and the fact that everyone's looking forward to the part of the gathering where they can begin drinking.

We snickered when we discovered that the musician the church had provided happened to be the exact guy Granddad loved to complain about every Sunday. "Ol' Strum and Mumble" he called him. And truly, the man couldn't stick to a melody if his life depended on it; the hymns he sung were unrecognizable to those of us who'd been singing hymns for a lifetime. You could almost see Granddad up there shaking his fist at the poor guy.

We held a huge bar-be-que at the ranch afterwards. Nearly everyone came from the church to reminisce about being chased after as kids and helped out, scolded and loved by my Granddad Charlie. It was good. By early evening, with the last of the mourners still spinning tales over picked over plates of beans and tri-tip, I was immobile on my grandmother's living room couch, too exhausted from grief and socializing to even lift my head. I had never expected that my months long low-grade sense of impending death could have been a portent to a *literal* funeral. I was truly ready to put a period on this run-on sentence of endings.

It was all I could do to stand up, but I had to finish packing if I was going to pull out of the driveway at 6:00 AM to meet my next beginning. Everyone would be sound asleep when I left, so I said my goodbyes. I walked the hundred yards down to my little apartment knowing that when I returned two weeks later, everything would feel different on the orchard. It made this road trip feel like a stolen blessing, a time to transition, a sacred moment for self, for processing, for moving into the reality of all this change. It was also a time to revel in the new truth that I had no obligations, no family counting on me any longer, no responsibilities. I was the least tethered I'd ever been. The freedom was heady.

I opened my front door and was greeted by sorted stacks of supplies and food and clothing just waiting to be tucked into duffels. *Well, let's get to it.* I began by dumping my purse out on my bed to repack it, and out tumbled the small cardboard box I'd purchased that morning. *Oh, shoot. Right.* I'd missed a cycle about a month into having sex with Jonah, but I hadn't thought much of it. He'd used protection, and I'd been known to miss cycles before. I'd taken a test just to be on the safe side. Negative. Anyway, Kat had told me hormones could get thrown all out of whack for a while the first time you have sex. I'd taken a second test two weeks later to be sure. Also negative.

It had been nearly three weeks since I'd last had sex, so I couldn't explain this morning's compulsion to stop by a Rite Aid on the way to the funeral to pick up yet another stick to pee on. I think I just wanted to shush the paranoid life-long-virgin-conditioned part of myself so that I could fully enjoy my trip without her nagging.

I dutifully marched off to the bathroom and peed on command. I'd gotten a different brand this time, like getting a second opinion. I set the stick to the side to do its thing and became again absorbed in the task at hand. I packed up duffels, loaded the car, and made a batch of cookies, lining them up on the sheet like regimental soldiers. I reviewed my packing list and dug around in my winter clothes for a hat that would keep me warm without making me look too idiotic. It wasn't until I surveyed the now empty living room, the last of the cookies in their tin and the last bag in the car, that I remembered the cheap plastic harbinger of fate perched on the edge of my bathroom sink. Without ceremony, I walked back into the bathroom and took a perfunctory look.

One little word rewrote in an instant the sense of new beginning I'd been carrying within me. None of it had been a metaphor. I was the cycle of death and birth personified. I had buried my grandfather this morning. And this evening, I was pregnant.

There was a saying that could often be heard repeated around the yoga studio at that time: The present defines the past. That one word, *pregnant* redefined every 'fact' of the previous months. That flu I'd had and the resultant aversion to alcohol and coffee, and the non-stop crying and bone deep exhaustion that I'd attributed to my grief had in reality been markers of hormones and resources realigning with a new creative project.

Two days into our road trip, somewhere between Zion National Park and Bryce Canyon, I told Naomi about the positive test. She took it in stride, unruffled. "You know that whatever you decide to do, I'll support you. We'll all support you."

I cocked my head and looked at her quizzically, uncomprehending. "What I'm going to do? I...oh, OH! No, no! I'm having the baby!" Naomi smiled at my cartoonish bug-eyed reaction. "That hadn't even crossed my *mind*." I took interest in the fact that it really hadn't.

The two weeks of our trip took on a slippery, sacred quality as though I'd dropped out of ordinary life and into liminal space. Absorbed by long stretches of highways, breathtaking vistas, and climbs to what felt like the top of the Earth, I was held in a time between times. It was a gift of transition for my soul. Even as our Buddhist teacher repeatedly reminded us that motherhood was the most taxing of all dharma, Naomi, seated on the cushion next to me, would pointedly raise an eyebrow in my direction, making me laugh. No judgement. No stake in the game.

Two days after I returned home, I sat in a doctor's office waiting for confirmation more substantial than what I could get from a glitchy little piece of manufactured plastic. The blonde doctor who tapped on the door was in her fifties with a kind face and gentle countenance.

"Well, the test is positive."

"Okay."

"We can set up an ultrasound. Do you know the last day of your last cycle?"

I told her. "It was my 30th birthday."

"So," the doctor hesitated, searching my face as she spoke the next words. "I'm thinking from your response that this is...welcomed... news?"

Tears instantly blurred my field of vison. I had to wait for the grip that seized my heart and throat to relax before I could speak. "I...I didn't expect it...I was a virgin...now I'm pregnant." As though that explained everything.

I left the office with an order for an ultrasound and prenatal vitamins. As soon as I reached the haven of my car, I dialed Naomi. "I've been waiting for your call! How are you?"

"Well," my voice went froggy with tears, "I see why this is meant to be done with a partner."

"Oh!" She despaired, "I almost got in the car and just drove over there and showed up, but I thought you'd think that was weird!"

I laugh-sobbed, "No! No, I would have loved that!"

Data Analysis:

It's not unusual for us to become focused on the endings in our lives. The feelings of loss from those who disappear grab our attention. I think this is in part because we assume that with their leaving, our access to the love they inspire in us will go fallow.

I'd assumed my opportunities to love were being removed, that I would need to go out and find new people that would inspire my love. My friends had gone, my grandfather had died. But now there was a child. It made me stop and wonder whether there had ever really been a time in my life where my capacity to love had gone unmet.

It was a question I continued to consider as Naomi drove me to the ultrasound where, through shared tears of wonder, we saw this new vessel of love for the first time in grainy black and white. I was eleven and a half weeks pregnant. Those two negative tests I'd taken six weeks earlier had been wrong. Very wrong. This baby had been conceived just after my thirtieth birthday, at my most infertile point, while using protection, with the first and only person I'd ever had sex with. The sheer impossibility of the whole thing reassured me; there was no question that I was in the throes of a masterful plan not of my own making.

Naomi held my hand in the car on the way home. I leaned back in the seat and watched her, my other palm already finding its instinctive resting place above my naval. I was overcome by affection for my friend. The flood of emotion felt like an answer to my inquiry. Maybe it isn't a matter of who shows up to ignite love within us. Maybe all we have to do is love, and someone will always appear to receive it.

Conclusion:

Love, like energy, can be neither created nor destroyed. It is not bound up in another being nor external force. Our experience of love lives in the closed loop system of self. The departure of a beloved, the arrival of another are not, though it may feel like it, generating love anew. That love is in us, was always in us, continues to be in us. Maybe certain people just happen to help us access it more easily.

I'm not being new age or theoretical here. The feeling of love is, like everything else, a collection of sensations in the body. We can identify where in our physical being we experience a change when someone we love walks into a room—a swelling in our chests, a tunnel vision, a grip of the stomach, an expansion of breath or involuntary contraction of the face into a smile. An external force can wield absolute power over these physical responses no more than it can take our ability to digest or breathe or pump blood through our veins. Love is ours to embody or not. And like any muscle, it benefits from practice.

There is, perhaps no chapter in this book in which a lesson can be communicated more readily through the experience of it. I encourage you to spend time in the experiment that follows. It's adapted from one of the very first meditations I learned at the yoga studio, and it remains one of my favorites.

Run Your Own Experiment No. 8:

The purpose of this experiment is to observe our feelings within loving relationship so that we can uncover expanded options and opportunities to access love independent of outside forces.

Experimental Procedure

1. Think of a being for whom you have easy affection. (*Note the word 'easy' here. Do not choose the person you're supposed to love or you want to love or with whom you have a complicated type of love. If no relationship of easy affection comes immediately to mind, I suggest you envision the smile of a friend's infant, the friendly neighbor's pet, or a fuzzy duckling.*)

2. Close your eyes.

3. Envision this being in your mind. Sit with them. Enjoy being in their presence.

4. Track the physical sensations you experience while in this being's presence.

5. Open your eyes and list the physical sensations you experience while feeling easy affection.

Take note that this being had to do nothing to elicit these feelings within you. You are the one who called the sensations up in your body at will. We all have the ability to call forth loving feelings anytime we wish, regardless of another's external participation.

Bonus Steps

1. Repeat steps one to four above.

2. Maintaining the physical experience of love, gently allow the image of this being to fade away.

3. If you begin to lose the physical feeling, call the image back.

4. Repeat this until you're able to let the image fade completely and still feel love in your body.

5. Practice recalling this feeling of love throughout your day.

CHAPTER NINE
Human Beings are not Scientific Constants

con·trol /kən'trōl/:
or control variable; the experimental element which
remains constant and unchanged throughout the
course of the scientific investigation.

SUBJECT: Overthinker; Female; Age 30 years, 2 months, 27 days.

HYPOTHESIS: Those genetically connected to me and my
child will automatically feel love and responsibility towards us as
dictated by deep human tribal patterns and powerful biological
imperative.

METHOD: Honor, awe, accusations.

FIELD SITE: My safe little apartment, the guesthouse of doom.

Experiment 140.70.1:

It had been a week since the doctor confirmed I was pregnant. Jonah had already been planning to visit town over the Fourth of July weekend, so I waited to tell him in person. It felt correct, respectful, to tell him face to face rather than over the phone. He was scheduled to arrive at my house at 8:00 AM. I felt the weight of holding such potentially life changing news. It was a big thing telling someone they were going to have a child. I was doing my best to get it right.

Jonah arrived on my doorstep looking worse for wear. "Hey! How are you?"

After a quick hug, he crossed the room and landed with a thud on my couch. "Ugh. Hungover. And exhausted."

"Do you want some coffee?"

"That'd be great. So, how was your roadtrip to Wyoming? What's going on?"

I'd been insistent with Jonah that we get together as soon as he got into town. I was determined to tell him before my parents who would be arriving later that afternoon. That too felt like the honorable order of events. Now that the moment was here, my nerves were on edge, and I was not quite ready to change his world yet. "You go first. Tell me how last night went." He'd gotten together with a friend. I listened, preoccupied, but as I'd hoped, the longer he talked, the more I calmed down. I eventually landed on the couch facing him cross-legged cradling my decaf cup of tea as he came to the summation: that he'd stayed up late into the night talking and drinking whiskey, thus the hangover.

"So, anyway, tell me, what's going on with you?" Again he asked, "How was your trip?"

I placed my mug on the coffee table to my left. "The trip was great. But, the reason I wanted to talk to you was because I wanted to tell you that I... well, I am pregnant."

Jonah's eyes widened and flitted over my body. "It's mine?"

"Yes."

He leaned in and put a hand on my only slightly protruding belly, just staring at it. "Wow." The expression was pure awe.

I laughed. "I know."

"Can I..." he gestured at my shirt.

"Oh, yeah. Of course." I leaned back against the pillow I'd propped behind me and rolled my up my tank top to reveal a slightly fuller stomach. He placed both hands against my skin in reverence. "I'm three months in. Through my first trimester. Everything looks fine so far. I just had it confirmed by the doctor last week, and I wanted to tell you in person." I told him in fits and starts about how I'd found out, how that flu I'd thought I'd had was really the baby, the fact that I had asked my parents to visit for the 4th of July and would be telling them the next day, pausing every now and again to let it all sink in, to sit together at the strangeness of it all.

"So, I'm due in January. And, listen, it's completely up to you how involved you want to be in the pregnancy process. If you want to come to appointments and that kind of thing just let me know. And more than that, really, it's your decision how involved you want to be with *any* of this. You know, whether you want to co-parent or don't want to be a parent, or whatever. I'm open to whatever you want to do. I just felt you should at least know."

"I really appreciate that."

"I don't have any expectations here. Really, I'm completely okay if you don't want your life to change in this way." I meant every word. When I'd tried to envision having children in the past, I'd always just seen snowy TV static. But then I'd discovered I was pregnant, and it hadn't seemed so outlandish. In fact, it almost felt like it made sense in some strange way. I began to wonder whether my inability to consider having a child had been based on the assumption that I'd have to have a husband as well.

Jonah, on the other hand, had always thought he was going to have kids. When he'd passed forty-five still a bachelor, he'd told me how strange it was having to come to terms with the fact that that wasn't going to be the case. He was still wearing a look of amazement, and his voice had a sort of floaty tone to it. My anxiety about telling him was a faint memory. "I...I probably need to go now. I have a 10:00."

"Yeah, of course. Go."

"But let's talk more."

"Definitely. I know this is just the beginning of the conversation. Let me get through telling my parents tomorrow, okay? We'll get together after."

"Yeah." He moved to the door but turned before walking out. "Hey, Kristen. I want you to know I'm not a guy who walks away. I step up. I'm going to step up."

His dramatic tone made me laugh. It was like he was repeating a line from a movie script. "I know, Jonah."

"I'm going to step up." He kept saying it bigger and more boldly as he walked to his car. I stood in the doorway smiling as he drove away.

The next afternoon Jonah texted.

> JONAH: Hey, I want to talk. Can you come over here?
>
> KRISTEN: I'm telling my parents in 2 hours. Let me get through that, and I'll come over tomorrow.
>
> JONAH: Okay. Good luck today.

The next day I drove the winding road up the hill to the address he'd given me. He was staying just a few blocks away from The Elk's Ear.

> KRISTEN: I'm here.

Jonah materialized on the side of the home and gestured for me to follow him. The side path opened into a large backyard with a tastefully designed pool and cabana with an incredible view. I followed him up the stone steps through the French doors of the guesthouse. The sense that something was off washed through me and set me on edge. Why did I feel like I was being brought to the principal's office to be given a talking to?

The guesthouse was a single large room with a sleeping loft on the second floor. The windows were floor to ceiling, but somehow the sun didn't manage to get in and brighten the place. Instead the space felt a vast, dank cave. "Do you want some water or anything?"

"Yeah, sure, I'll take some water." Jonah's demeanor seemed changed from 48 hours earlier. I took a seat on the couch and felt myself watching him, waiting for clues as to what was coming next, sensing his movements and tracking them as prey tracking an unfamiliar predator. He placed the water on the coffee table in front of me, but rather than joining me on the couch, he retreated to a stuffed chair in the corner of the room as far from me as he could get without physically leaving the building. He held himself like a wounded animal, his face haunted, his eyes never making contact with mine. He was totally unfamiliar to me. My mind kept searching for recognizable notes of my friend, the person I cared for and trusted, the person who'd made me feel safe, accepted, supported. But that person wasn't in this room with us. Fear seeped into my bones. Something was very wrong.

"So, I'll be honest, I don't remember anything from a couple of days ago. I think I went into shock the moment you told me." I remained silent, not sure what he expected by way of response. "I've been in the belly of the whale these last two days. I've done a lot of crying and soul searching. And the more I've thought about it, the less it makes any sense to me. I don't understand how this happened. I was careful."

My mind flashed to the image of him over me, laughing like a schoolboy who'd just played a funny joke when he'd pushed himself slightly into me after asking whether he could just press the tip so I could see how it felt. *"We just had seeex!"*

I kept quiet. Frozen. My whole being braced.

"And, I've been on the phone these last two days—with family, friends, my therapist—I've been talking to a lot of people breaking down, crying, trying to get a handle on this. And, you know, a few of them asked me a question that has stuck with me. They asked me whether you could have tricked me into getting pregnant. Like, you wanted a baby and wanted to have my baby."

The fear bloomed outward from my marrow and into my muscles where it entered the bloodstream and transformed to horror, confusion, and disbelief. My mind attempted to catch up with what was happening. The turnaround was too fast for me to process real time. I remained still on the couch, slipping into survival mode.

"And, you know, there was this one night near the end when I saw one of the used condoms on the floor and something told me to pick it up and take it with me because you might use it to … well, to inseminate yourself."

I could taste bile in the back of my throat.

"And I remember you saying that for all you knew, you were going to end up with a woman someday, and I began to think that you might have done that, used one of my old condoms to get yourself pregnant, so that you could have this nice little family. You know, with Naomi or something."

I went numb. Stared at him blankly. He was grasping at straws, and now he was taking our most intimate conversations, the emotional musings that had been allowed only because our friendship had been the safest of containers, and he was twisting them in service of a fiction he was spinning to get himself out of this. Not to walk away—I gave him that option free and clear—but to absolve himself of having had any part, any responsibility for his actions. He had his narrative laid out, the one that allowed him to still see himself as a 'good guy.' And not only had he cast me as the witch to be burned at the stake, but he was using the other most important, safe relationship in my life as kindling. My friend Jonah was gone. He had died. Whoever this stranger was, he was a threat.

"I want you to take a paternity test."

I couldn't believe what he was asking. My words came out as a whisper, "You are the only person I've ever slept with. You know that."

"Well, I don't know, maybe there was your friend David."

What was he *talking* about? Tears of humiliation began to stream down my face.

"I think maybe then this will all seem more real to me, if I can see a piece of paper that says this really is my child."

I was at a loss. Broken. Small. I nodded just to make it stop.

"I mean, I don't know if it was a tactic to not tell me about the pregnancy until it was too late to...to *do* anything about it." He must have seen my face change. *This man wants to reach into my body and kill my child. Engage immediate lockdown.* "And, I don't even know that that would have been something you'd have done anyway—"

"No." My voice was unequivocal, stony despite the flow of tears. My entire body, in fact was turning to stone. The drawbridges coming up, his access to me closing off for good. "It isn't."

"Right, I get that. It's just... you didn't even give me the chance to have that conversation with you. I didn't even get to talk to you about it. That just seems calculated."

"I didn't know for sure myself until ten days ago." Some part of me was still under the illusion that I was in a rational conversation.

"Right. Yeah." He didn't hear me. My responses had no impact; they just slid right off of him. The story he'd crafted for himself was bullet-proof. Truth was unimportant now.

"And I'd like you to not say anything to anybody. I know some of your friends must already know, but don't tell anyone else you're pregnant. I haven't told my girlfriend yet, and I don't want her to find out from someone else. Her circles cross with the people from your yoga studio."

He'd started dating a woman in town just before he'd moved away. I was suddenly fearful he would discover the handful of my friends who already knew. Did he have control over who I told about the state of my body? "How long will it be before you tell her?"

"I don't know. Maybe a week."

"A *week*?"

"I just need some time to figure out how to tell her. I mean," His voice slipped into a therapist affect, as though he were reciting recommended treatments from an ADA manual, "you should have your support system around you, of course. Just don't go telling everyone."

When would this be over? I was trapped, shut down, withstanding each blow, just surviving the encounter. I became numb. I'd stopped taking in his version of reality as he continued to talk, telling me what I was doing wrong, explaining to me how this whole situation was my fault, and how he magnanimously was choosing to not hold that against me.

I had considered before telling him that Jonah might not be around to help with the child, that he might choose a different looking life, one without the complication of fatherhood, but I had never expected him to be cruel to me, to sit me down and explain to me that I was a liar and a whore. I couldn't have anticipated this withdrawal of caring and kindness, this rewrite of our history. Our friendship had been vital to me. The fact that we'd engaged in sex for a few weeks before he'd moved away had simply been a footnote to our relationship in my mind, just one more realm in which I'd felt safe to question and explore with him. He had even thanked me at the end, citing our physical encounter as the thing that had broken him of his jadedness, that had allowed him to be open and receptive to dating again. How could he so easily toss aside the safe container I thought we'd built together?

Jonah held me there for over an hour, an emotional hostage, a child being restrained by a tyrannical parent. I left in tears, feeling dirty, shamed, like garbage tossed aside. I felt I'd been raped, my emotions, my memories, my reality taken from me against my will.

Jonah had turned on me. It would be six months before my parents would be able to look at me without wincing. Thank God I had someone to turn to who would greet me with love and acceptance. I steered my car back down the mountain, flipped my blinker, and turned left towards Naomi's house.

Data Analysis:

The people who can love us are not necessarily the people who are 'supposed to' love us. When I discovered I was pregnant, I unconsciously assumed that the people who would rally around me were supposed to be blood, my parents, the baby's father. Out of a kind of deep Neolithic part of the brain I'd automatically turned to them first in deference to some amorphous claim of genetics and lineage. I had expected our loving history to imply a loving future. I had been under the impression that because Jonah had shown me care he would continue to act with care. I had assumed that he would love the child inside of me because it was his DNA. Because he should. But I learned the reality, quite jarringly, that no one owed me, or my child for that matter, love.

No one owes us love. Waking up to that reality can shake us to our cores, but it can also, in an instant, free us. By knocking us out of our constructed illusions of how things are supposed to work in matters of love and parenting and partnership, our hands are no longer unknowingly tied. We are allowed to stand up amidst the emotional rubble, blinking the dust from our eyes, and scan the newly flattened landscape for what is real, to discover who is still standing, who, in fact, is standing right alongside us.

It wasn't until all of my emotional and practical supports got knocked out from under me that I could clearly see who actually *was* there loving me, not who was *supposed* to be. The yogis, Naomi, my childhood girlfriends, the blue-haired at church, total strangers. And in seeing it, in recognizing love's unsolicited reason-less flow toward me, miracle of miracles, because I had no choice, I was able to accept it. I needed their support.

Conclusion:

Love plays a reverse game of hide and seek with us. We count to ten, open our eyes, and though she's standing in the middle of the room in plain sight, we hurry to the crawlspace to see if, perhaps, she's waiting for us there. Love is not a scarce resource, we simply are in the habit of looking for her in all the wrong places.

There's this one story that my friend and former business partner tells often. It was back when his band was on the rise, playing arenas, touring with Pink and Coldplay, doing Conan. By all accounts, he'd already reached a level of success few aspiring musicians ever touch, but he was so focused on chasing some specific idyllic accolade, some confirmation of his stardom, that he was missing it. "We had just finished a show, and this woman came up to me after to tell me how much she loved us and what a huge difference our music had made in her life. And I remember vividly the moment that I caught myself looking past her into the crowd, half listening as she bared her soul, wondering if any record labels had shown up. When I realized what I was doing I was horrified." We all have had this experience at some level—we're unable to see the adoration, support, the love that already is because we're too busy standing on our tiptoes, looking over her head, searching for her.

I should know, I'm a product of that pattern. After my mother first met my father she completely counted him out, convinced he was too straight laced, too ambitious, too unlike all the men she'd ever dated. It was over a year later that they met again, and she could see what was in front of her, and they married just six months later and just celebrated their 36th wedding anniversary.

We have such clear ideas of the packaging in which love 'should' arrive, that we blow past the willing, generous, flow from the unexpected source. We pigeonhole love, make her smaller and more limited. But Love is brash and adamant and will not be boxed up. She takes many forms, and if we open our awareness to that, we discover she's never far, and she has big plans for us. Love chooses her own messengers.

Run Your Own Experiment No. 9:

The purpose of this experiment is to broaden our vision to incorporate all available inflows of love so that we might recognize unexpected opportunities for receiving support from others.

Experimental Procedure:

1. Make a list of everyone who is supposed to love you in this life—parents, siblings, that friend you've had since grade school, your dog, your kids, your spouse—all of them.

2. Next to each name, write why they are supposed to love you.

3. Now, imagine you end up in jail or the hospital or receive bad news. Or good news. Who are your first calls when you get a promotion, see a funny greeting card, have a really great date? Close your eyes and really put yourself in situations of sorrow, need, and joy, and discover whose number you start to dial.

4. Write these names down.

5. Compare your lists. Are the people on your second set of lists also on your first? They very well may be. And they very well may not. And either is totally fine. What's important is to be aware of the vast sources and many directions love and support and partnership are already present in our lives.

CHAPTER TEN
Like Attracts Like

at·tract /əˈtrakt/:
to cause to approach or adhere; to pull or draw
toward oneself; to draw by appeal to natural or
excited interest, emotion, or aesthetic

SUBJECT: Overthinker; Female; Age 28 years, 9 months, 24 days.

HYPOTHESIS: My relationships to this point have not fit well within pre-established bounds of societal categorization; my 'romantic' relationships have not been romantic enough, and my platonic relationships have been too intimate. Therefore, I need to either artificially restrict or inflate my bonding behaviors to have successful normal relationships in the future.

METHOD: Yoga, cellular technology, mind-melding.

FIELD SITE: The daily life culminating in a cheery if chilly delivery room.

Experiment 130.10.04:

Naomi and I met just five months before I left the insurance job and eighteen months before I found myself pregnant. As part of a multi-directional strike plan to make friends, I had taken up yoga at a sweet studio near the beach. (Also part of this plan were tennis lessons, committing to a regular church service, and pointedly sitting alone at the bar of a local pub to make myself conspicuously available for conversation).

One morning I walked into the studio to find the scheduled instructor out sick. I was instead greeted at the door by a stranger who felt like anything but. She took my hand and welcomed me with such attention that it was as though she had divined the exact level of warmth, connection, and intimacy I desired for all of my dearest relationships and, rather than wasting time, simply started us there.

Now, generally speaking I am not terribly observant of people. Patterns, structures, details and landmarks, these I seem to record more thoroughly than most, but the mess of humanity usually registered only as the fuzzy obstacle to look beyond. Conversations like this were commonplace in my world:

Friend: Did you see that cute guy sitting behind us on the plane?
Me: No.
Friend: He was part of the Australian soccer team that took over the whole back of coach.
Me: There was a soccer team on the plane?
Friend: They were literally wearing day-glo soccer jerseys.
Me: Huh. No kidding.
Friend: <exasperated eye roll>

This natural state of not-seeing laid a background that contrasted starkly with those few times I actually did take note of an individual. Amidst the sea of hazy people-blob, suddenly a face would emerge clearly as though caught in a spotlight, and I could *see* her. And with that seeing, that recognizing, I accepted that the clock had started on our story, our friendship begun, we were now yoked in some cosmic fashion that was, as of yet, a mystery.

Something deep in me recognized Naomi from the get go. Internally, that is. Externally she was unlike anyone I'd known growing up in the suburbs of Chicago. Not yet forty, greying dirty blond hair juxtaposed with her unlined make-up-less face to gave her what I came to think of as an air of Eternal Yogic Wisdom. She wore embroidered Indian kurtas, flowing pants, and methodically wrapped her mala beads around her wrist as she opened each class. She was the consummate den mother, hugging and kissing (on the lips, I was alarmed and thrilled to note) each person who came through the door, immediately committing to memory newcomers' names. I came to anticipate the moment her eyes characteristically slipped closed while giving a dharma talk only to unexpectedly snap open and connect so strongly with my own gaze as to make me acutely aware of the fact that I'd spent a lifetime never having truly looked anyone in the eye.

Her otherness was further confirmed the first time she invited me to her home. The way she lived was so foreign I simply didn't know what to make of it at first. I was twenty-eight, Naomi thirty-nine. Where I was from, reaching the age of thirty-nine meant you had a healthy retirement fund, owned a house in a nice neighborhood, had invested in some grown-up furniture, dishware, and whatever other creature comforts you valued. Naomi lived in a haphazard feeling space with windows that never seemed to latch and no true furniture to speak of. In the kitchen, there wasn't enough space for a table and chairs, so they remained shoved against a corner until needed. Her dishes of gifted handmade pottery were stacked in crazy, precarious piles on the baker's rack that acted as cabinetry, and from what I could tell, not a single piece of her silverware came from a matching set.

The items that made up Naomi's wardrobe arrived from India every six months wrapped in seemingly incidental bits of paper, tape, and string and covered in mysterious Hindi markings. Nearly everything she surrounded herself with felt exotic to me. The only indication that she had arrived in this home in this life from via a traditional middle-America corporate career so many years earlier was the massive computer screen perched on top of a thick hardback yoga reference book and her quietly obsessive need to own the latest smartphone. On more than one occasion I watched her shatter yet another iPhone screen and wondered if her stubborn refusal to use a case was really just her deeper self-demanding newer and shinier.

She was addicted to that phone. She always picked it up no matter what she was doing. I was soon trained into a Pavlovian rhythm when we were together. *Ding*—pause my sentence—phone down—continue what I was saying. On one hand, I found it irritating, but on the other hand, her love affair with that little screen allowed us to fall into an easy rhythm of constant and instant conversation from morning to night. Before long, even when she wasn't with me, she was, and I her.

From early on it was apparent that this woman was not my teacher, she was my practice-mate. The observations she shared in class, those that so deeply spoke to my experience, were not the parts of life she had already figured out—they were the seekings and struggles and lessons she was working through in that very moment. We were both searching. I felt the respect she held for the shape of my seeking. She spoke it plainly, genuinely thrilled when I would arrive on her doorstep still in my church dress. This was, at its root, the topic of all of our conversations—our one continuous conversation, really—the exploration of our meaning and purpose on the planet. I'd never encountered anyone so willing to jump in, open and unabashed in the search with me nor so fearlessly willing to share her ridiculous, ugly, and revealing data right alongside her insights, thereby allowing me to do the same.

I felt I'd found a comrade-in-arms. Nothing felt off limits, nothing too crazy or mundane to share, every heart-felt observation met with respectful consideration. It took me a while to get used to, actually. Naomi listened to me, and even more shockingly, she was actually interested in what I was saying! There was no built-in margin for the throwaway comments or filler sentences that made up most polite conversation. If I offhandedly dropped a phrase born of social graces into the mix, she took me at my word and wanted to know whether I could, please, expand on it. This made me realize two important things: 1. A shocking number of sentences that came out of my mouth through the course of a day were born of social graces, and 2. I wasn't used to someone actually paying attention to what I was saying.

I found I had to enter a new level of mindfulness, an even more committed practice of honesty. The practice of speaking only what was true to my experience and dropping those that were parroted or indefensible moved me into a new level of awareness. And the rigorous attention required fostered in me a new appreciation for silence. I learned to simply not speak when I had nothing to say. It was revolutionary!

In fact, the more time Naomi and I spent together the fewer words we needed to communicate. Our verbal interactions became more non-sensical to outsiders as our knowledge of one another became more exact. Sitting across the table in her home office, engrossed in the business of helping her organize volunteers, supplies, and schedules for the yoga conference her studio would be hosting, she'd suddenly blurt, "You know, on Tuesday," to which I'd respond something like, "Yeah, the papers," without lifting my head. Naomi would look up, pleased as punch. "We're so much more efficient now that we don't have to actually use words to communicate!"

The physical ease and affection available between us too was unlike any I'd ever hoped to encounter in adulthood. I happily aligned with her practice of kissing one another on the lips. There was always a hug, a hand on an arm, a back. We shared sleeping space easily when traveling, and conversations while standing undressed in the bathroom or with our heads tilted toward one another at the Korean spa were commonplace. There was no conditioned shyness or pre-apologizing for our physical forms. There was no dearth of compliments when she was having a good boob day or my arms were looking particularly toned at the gym. We felt strong and beautiful together.

We enhanced one another's lives in all sorts of small ways. We were good influences on each other—she cut down on swearing, while two of my favorite vices, television and wine, became such infrequent companions that I considered selling my TV altogether. Her taste in clothes edged towards mine. My taste in reading leaned towards hers. People began to ask if we were sisters. A large family visiting from China stopped us to take their picture one day on a hike and promptly informed us we had, 'same face.' We ended every phone call, every live encounter, and texted it throughout the day with 'I love you.' When I pulled up my messenger, the logarithm anticipated my first word as a choice of 'I', 'love', or 'Naomi'.

Perhaps my favorite part of all of it was the way we fell into perfect companionship in the mundane. I drove her to the airport, enjoying the uninterrupted hours of intimate time together sitting in the gridlock of the 405 interstate. We bought groceries for one another. When she took her family snorkeling over the holidays, they put me down as the emergency contact for the whole family. She borrowed my clothes. We selfied our outfits for approval before going out. She cooked breakfast for us most mornings, and some days, lunch and dinner as well. We bought one another gifts and never bought ourselves a cupcake or a green juice without also bringing one back for the other. I'd leave her after spending four hours together, and five minutes later my phone would ring, "I know I just saw you, but I have to tell you what just happened..." We'd care for one another when we were sick—she with soup, I drawing from my armament of Western medicine. Going to the bank together, standing in line at the DMV, everything made more pleasant because we were spending time together.

It was on one of our morning walks that I was struck by how much I'd come to trust our relationship, to rely on it. We were walking along side by side in comfortable silence, the sound of our feet on the asphalt, the waking birds, the helicopter-beat of the wind machines warding off the chill in the surrounding orchards our shared meditation. I found myself in wonder at the deep satisfaction I felt, warm and full of the ease of being there, present with my friend, sharing the simple act of being with. I'd never cultivated so diligent and deep a practice of being with anyone before, and I could see that being with her in this way was allowing me to be with myself in new ways as well. Just an hour earlier I had been lying in bed, my mind preparing and planning, cataloguing the day, but the moment Naomi and I embraced in the driveway, all the monkeys went quiet. I wasn't in the future of imagination or worry, nor the past of regret and analysis, but right here, on this road, taking this step, listening to her breathing alongside my own, one breath at a time. Deeply content. I had the sense that she was the welcome anchor that tethered me to my very being.

"I like myself when I'm with you."

She looked at me, genuinely touched. "That's the best compliment you've ever given me."

When I found out I was pregnant, I was nervous that it would mean an end not only to our closeness but to my place in my community of yoga friends. Finding this tribe had been like stumbling upon water in the desert. A group of women in their late thirties and forties, mostly divorced or so long in their marriages that they never mentioned their husbands, all actively seeking something, gathering joyfully and affectionately, encouraging one another in their pursuits. I was anxious that these friends would, understandably, I felt, leave me behind to motherhood. But the vacuum of anticipated support in which I found myself was filled to overflowing by the love and joy offered by these exact women, none more loudly than Naomi.

Without fanfare, she became my person, my go to, my primary partner. Now empty after Granddad's death, I moved into my grandparents' house, and Naomi moved near enough to call me 'neighbor.' Always appreciative of our physical ease and affection she now became witness to the bizarre ways my body changed. (*Kristen:* You seriously have to come over here and check out my pelvis. *Naomi:* On my way!) She got misty eyed with me the first time we saw the baby's fluttering heart on the ultrasound screen and stood beside me as the nurse told us I was going to have a little boy. She witnessed my awe the first time I felt him move in my belly in protest of a posture I'd taken on the yoga mat.

As we left the studio one afternoon, she looked me over, "You look different. Are we having a baby tonight?"

"Noooo. C'mon. I'm fine. I'll see you tomorrow."

My water broke at 4:00 AM. I texted Naomi.

> KRISTEN: You need to get a sub today. We're going to be busy birthing a baby.

She responded immediately.

> NAOMI: What do you need? Are you okay? Should I come over?

> KRISTEN: I'm fine, my water just broke. I'm going to let my mom sleep and try to get a few more hours of rest myself. I'll call the doctor at 7:00. I want to keep that appointment to get the car detailed and wrap up a few work things. Plan on heading up to the hospital around noon.

A few minutes after noon Naomi, my mother, and I met in my driveway for the short trek up the mountain to the hospital. Our local hospital was too small to handle deliveries, so we headed one town over. It felt a little like we were off to summer camp for some big adventure. We stopped along the way and posed at the lookout point, my big belly perched on our town sign, the view of our valley stretching behind. Once at the hospital, I put on my gown and rolled myself like a beached whale onto the hospital bed. Naomi took up position at the foot of the bed and reassuringly placed her hands firmly on my feet while they hooked me up to machines. Other family members arrived. All of us were abuzz with excitement, cracking jokes and entertaining one another as doctors and nurses flitted in and out.

"Are you having much pain from the contractions?" One doctor interjected.

"Oh, no. I never started them. My water broke around 4:00 AM, but the contractions never came."

The doctor looked up from the long readout she held in her hands. "Oh, you're definitely having contractions. You're not feeling them at all? They're coming about every six minutes. Pretty strong too."

The doctor's words were met with stunned silence. Then Naomi let out a laugh, "Of course you're not feeling them! This is how your entire pregnancy has been!" It was true. I'd had the smoothest pregnancy in the world, and we were about to find out what kind of delivery it would be. My primary came in to do a final ultrasound. The baby had moved out of position just a few weeks earlier, and we'd all been waiting to see whether he'd flip himself back around. She confirmed that he was still feet down. He'd be a breech C-section delivery just like I'd been.

The nurses came to wheel me into the surgical theatre, and they whisked Naomi off to change into scrubs. I'd never had any sort of surgery before and came into the surgical suite shivering. "Is this nerves, or am I cold?" I asked the kind looking nurse who had her arms wrapped around me while the anesthesiologist administered the spinal block.

"Oh, honey, you *are* shivering." She laid me back and covered me with one of those silver sheets you see rescue workers use. The shivering stopped, and the bizarre experience of losing sensation below the chest kicked in. I could hear the doctors coming in, chatting easily with the nurses. They were asking something about the anesthesiologist's wife.

When they brought Naomi in to stand up by my head, she leaned in and said, "It feels so nice and friendly in here." I felt the same. It was almost all women. Everyone was relaxed. It felt like I was in good hands.

Naomi watched the whole procedure over the screen they'd

placed at my chest and gave me the play by play. "Okay, they've just made the cut. And now they have—wow, they have your whole uterus out. You have a lovely uterus. Really." She looked down at me smiling, and I laughed. "It looks like they're about to –"

"Why, hello!" I heard one of the doctors' voices from the other side of the screen.

"Oh, he's out, and his eyes are wide open! He just looked right at the doctor!" Suddenly, Naomi stepped back, and in her place appeared gloved hands holding my son. He disappeared again behind the screen to be cleaned up, and Naomi returned to my left side.

They returned with my son and laid him on my chest while they finished putting me back in one piece. When it was time to wheel me to recovery, Naomi stayed with the baby and held him on her skin until it was time for him to be checked by the nurses. The baby was healthy, responding, and nearly ten pounds.

I stayed in the hospital for three nights getting to know this new little soul in my life. Naomi stayed with us over one of those night and visited daily, sometimes crawling into bed next to me to just share in the awe. Once home, she was my tether to the outside world, to work, to normalcy as I rode the waves of physical, emotional, and psychological transition into motherhood. I both loved my son and felt loved by Naomi in ways I couldn't have imagined.

"You know," she ventured as we were on the phone one evening, "I was thinking, if there were some sort of ceremony for us...I just don't know what it would look like." She trailed off, and I broke into an unseen grin. Her ability to reach into my brain and speak my thoughts never ceased to leave me stunned.

"I know. I've thought the same." I'd thought it had been a crazy, too-much, silly thought, but Naomi had again been right there with me. Ahead of me. Braver than I in calling out just how important our relationship was. How sacred and deserving of sanctity. Naomi and I had found in one another someone to match our unique vision of intimate relationship. My heart swelled. It felt held, full, and satiated.

Data Analysis:

I heard a social scientist on the radio once cite his four-year-old daughter as the inspiration for his study of humans' approach to relationship. While driving his daughter and her new playmate through town, he witnessed their exchange. It went something to the effect of: I like pizza. *I like pizza.* I like ice cream. *I like ice cream.* I love popcorn. *I love popcorn.* I don't like ice cream. *I don't like ice cream.* He realized that what was happening was not so much a declaration of genuine soul-felt likes and dislikes (as proven by the girls' ambivalent stance on ice cream), but rather a probing and confirming that both parties were interested in finding commonalities and, thereby, building relationship.

As children exploring connection from the ground up, we are all natural born scientists. Every reaction and bit of feedback from others is quickly analyzed and integrated. Each interaction holds a formative power in shaping the way we approach relationship throughout our lives.

Growing up I was often deemed 'too much,' and even as an adult I'm often likened to a Labrador Retriever in my full-on enthusiastic affection for those I adore. I received the message early that my intensity in relationship, my loyalty and fierceness, my physicality and desire to be so intimate with another who was not a designated romantic partner, was strange or inappropriate. In Naomi, I found someone who not only accepted my behavior but met it, matched it, even one upped it. *I like yoga.* Me too. *I like holding hands with my friends.* Me too. *I like cooking.* I like eating your cooking. *I like talking about the meaning of the universe.* Me too!

Through many missteps, I finally learned that in all things intimate, intention is key. Physical connection, affectionate touch, kissing, even being comfortable skin to skin, none of these held sexual charge for me, yet the assumption that they did had so often been unleashed upon me that I'd become self-conscious in relationship. It had made me feel shamed and secretive, and at times threatened to cut me off entirely from the type of platonic, joyful, physical human connection I craved. The pure joy and absolute relief at finding in Naomi another human being whose ideas of what an intimate relationship could look like matched my own was positively thrilling. For the first time I caught a glimmer of what others must see in the idea of partnering. I could begin to envision a type of relationship that would add to my life's purpose rather than drag on it, and it was nothing I could have described in a match.com profile.

My experience with Naomi showed me that the fact that I didn't desire any of the types of partnership I saw modeled around me didn't necessarily mean I was destined to be without companionship altogether. It just meant I had to find a like-mind. And it appeared I had.

Conclusion:

A physicist in New Zealand made a discovery in 2012 that flew in the face of everything we'd known about electrostatics. He observed that when two positively charge spheres get close enough to one another they actually began to affect the distribution of one another's charged particles such that rather than repel, they became attracted to each other. The physical phenomenon reminded me of something I'd read about brainwaves in human relationship. "In the very moment that you experience positivity resonance [i.e. love], your brain syncs up with the other person's brain…you and the other are on the same wavelength. As your respective waves mirror one another, each of you—moment by moment—changes the other's mind."*

As illustrated by the chatter of two four-year-olds in the back seat of a car, half of the battle of finding satisfying relationship is in finding a willing participant, someone who is interested in playing, in finding a version of relationship that is satisfying for both parties. And what both physics and neuroscience seem to be

---

* Paris, Dr. Jeannette. *Heartbreak*

pointing towards is the fact that once we've entered that agreement, once we've begun to move closer to one another, our likenesses, our attraction in the beginning stages of building relationship, will naturally gain momentum. Like attracts like, and then the likes become more alike.

Perhaps it is hopeful thinking on my part, but I'm going to posit that there is no limit to what relationship can look like. We can craft a human to human container shaped any way we want it, that satisfies our deepest needs and/or most pie in the sky desires, so long as we find someone willing to enter the experiment with us. To find that person, we have to put out the call, we have to speak honestly about what we want out of a relationship.

The first step in connecting with someone who wants the same type of relationship we do is getting clear about what we want. Forget the judgement and what's allowed. Let's build our perfect partnership from the ground up.

Run Your Own Experiment No. 10:

The purpose of this experiment is to expand our view of relationship beyond the boundaries held by the culture, community, and friends currently impacting our world view so that we can craft a more personally satisfying image of partnership.

Experimental Procedure:

1. On a piece of paper, list all of the characteristics you'd like a primary partnership (or any other type of relationship you'd like to work with) to contain. It might be useful to review your lists from Experiment 5 as you begin. (*Note: This is a list about qualities of partnership, not a potential partner.*)

2. Once complete, read through your list and cross out any items that were written in deference to something other than your personal innate desires. (*Note: For me, a good meter for this is*

whether I spontaneously imagine my father, a judgmental friend, or the whole of society standing over my shoulder reading the item along with me and nodding approvingly.)

3. Consider now, what items you may have left off this list. What felt too audacious, silly, or Pollyanna to include? What are the things you haven't allowed yourself or feel like you're doing it wrong? Add these items now.

4. Underline any quality that is currently being met in any of your relationships.

5. Now, take note of any qualities that are not underlined. Are these values shared or shunned by those you surround yourself with? Consider seeking like-minded individuals who also value one or more of these un-met qualities.

CHAPTER ELEVEN

Tune into Your
Intimacy Resonance

res·o·nance /ˈrezənəns/:
the reinforcement or prolongation of sound by
reflection or synchronous vibration of a neighboring
object

SUBJECT: Overthinker; Female; Age 31 years, 8 months.

HYPOTHESIS: Having discovered the white whale—another person whose language and style of intimacy and relationship matches my own—our shared resonance can only grow exponentially.

METHOD: Shared beds, sex, fence sitting.

FIELD SITE: The hundred-yard, no-man's-land between the tree line and Naomi's front door.

Experiment 151.11.5:

My mind roused to consciousness, but I remained still, eyes closed, only a creeping awareness of the rhythmic swoosh of my pulse in my eardrums; my body had not yet surrendered rest to the reality of wakefulness. The duvet held my limbs in place with a reassuring weight, and the crisp scentless-ness of the pillow under my head reminded me that I was in an unfamiliar bed. *Washington. The workshop begins today.* I could tell the sun was up through my closed lids but had no sense of time. The muffled sounds seeping through the cracked window were nature-born rather than man-made, so I posited that it was still early and let my body sink more deeply into its imprint.

The mattress shifted beside me. I cracked one eye open. A patch of smooth tanned skin filled my vision. The heavy white bedding had shifted in the night to reveal her bare shoulder, now three inches from my nose, close enough to feel my breath, I thought. My heart lightly gripped at the sight, jostling it out of its steady cadence of hibernation, and I was overcome with tenderness.

Her form lay beside me, but she herself had not yet returned from her nightly travels back to our little room. She was still out there somewhere, and I waited alone for her arrival, anticipating the reengagement of our connection. I tracked the sunrise by the way it lit each individual hair upon the mesmerizing slope of her shoulder before leaping to caress its way across her clavicle. My eyes followed its pioneering progression, the permission to be this close as satisfying as if it were my own fingers reverently tracing her skin.

In her absence, I missed 'us.' I shut my eyes to soften the wait by basking in the catalogue of storybook feelings that I had been introduced to through our friendship; the wonder at being someone's first thought, the thrill of permission given, the freedom afforded by an invitation and the exhilaration of stepping into fellowship to meet and be met. Having touched such intoxicating intermingling with another, found myself occasionally craving new modes of expression.

In response, my imagination closed the physical space between us, pressed my mouth against her now luminous skin, felt the gratifying firmness of her against the softness of my lips. I indulged, replaying the sensations a second time. A third.

My unconscious searched for other languages to more fully articulate the affection I felt. I allowed the next scene to unwind. Cozied in to my sleep-mate in the same manner I imagined dozens of others up and down this street to be, I looped one arm into the crook of her elbow and slid the other beneath the cool sheet, my palm like a starfish across the landscape of her smooth stomach. My right leg threaded itself familiarly between hers, communing in a tangle of limbs shiny and sun-kissed from hiking the day before. I conjured an appreciative, 'mmm,' her right hand moving to join mine and affirm its rightful home above her naval, her face reorienting towards me like a flower seeking sun. Our bodies in congress, resting in one another. I, feeling welcomed. Wanted. Happy.

She stirred next to me, and my thoughts returned from their alternate universe to this one. I opened my eyes to find her stretching her arms overhead, the duvet shrugged down to her waist. "Mmmmm… good morning." She smiled down at me and then snuggled back down under the warmth of the covers, turning towards me.

"Good morning," I smiled back and slipped my hand into hers offered between us. Our bare toes danced their friendly greeting to one another at the foot of the bed. My whole being took delight in the sweet, reassuring touch, the intimacy of this moment. The intimacy that felt like everything. "How'd you sleep?"

She scrunched her forehead searching for a memory. "I dreamed I was preparing to climb the Himalayas, and my mom had packed me a bag lunch for the journey. What about you?"

"Nothing I can remember." Satisfied, she threw the covers off the bed. "Geeze!" My bare skin exposed, the morning chill surprised me. Naomi laughed in response and swung her legs off the mattress. I took in the curve of her spine as she crossed to the bathroom and started the shower.

"Drgh yooo waat dogit goofffy?" She stood squarely in the doorway, looking at me expectantly, easy under my gaze, toothbrush buzzing away in her mouth. *This is intimacy.* These little tableaus never failed to leave me feeling privileged.

"I'm sorry," my tone landed somewhere between mockingly sincere and just plain mocking, "...was I supposed to understand that?"

She grinned and threw a hand towel at my head before disappearing for a moment to spit. "I said, do you want to get coffee?"

"As soon as possible." She stepped into the shower, and I dropped back into the pillows to wait my turn. I marveled that even the momentary barrier of a cheap plastic shower curtain could incite in me what felt like an almost cellular-level impatience to reunite. I mused over how much time and water would be saved if it were socially acceptable for friends to share showers. Call it ten minutes a day at x gallons a minute... it really would be the responsible thing to do.

"Your turn!" I pressed the heels of my hands to my eyes, blew a long, restrained breath out through puffed cheeks, and rolled out of bed. Thus began another day in Friendship Lab.

One of the reasons Naomi and I bonded early on was that neither dating nor sex ranked highly on our topics of interest. So, I was surprised and somewhat amused when Naomi confessed that she'd become newly aware of just how long it had been since she'd had sex. True to our soul-agreement, we did what we always did when a new aspect of self appeared, we invited it in and played with ways to get to know it better. She quickly located a willing male lab partner, and her daily reports of the previous night's experiments became a favorite new topic on our morning walks. She was an open book, and my clarifying questions were met with her usual thoughtful consideration. She did her best to illuminate this unknown planet and its inhabitants, and I did my best to grasp its foreignness.

Her renewed sex drive, which I came to understand had merely been in a state of hibernation since we'd met, had very little impact on our daily routine. I did occasionally find myself irritated when her anticipation of sex distracted from our work. Or when her focus on the object of her lust left me holding the bag of logistics that needed to be handled for one of *her* projects. And I couldn't help but resent her late night extracurriculars a little when she began missing our morning walks. But these were sacrifices made in the name of experimentation. After a couple of months, though, I began to notice her wardrobe subtly shifting. Her cooking took on new flavors, and she began to keep beer in her fridge. It wasn't until her sense of humor began to change that an uneasy feeling took up residence in the pit of my stomach. Her jokes became more crass, juvenile enough that I found myself cringing rather than laughing at times. My reaction didn't escape her notice, and she'd address it with a dismissive, "Oh, forget it, you have no sense of humor."

The first time I offered up observation of these small erosions, she quickly waved me off, unwilling to engage, adamant that she was just as she'd always been. I took the implication to be that she thought I was being either too sensitive or crazy. I wanted to be seen as neither, so I witnessed quietly from then on. I willfully fought back the waves of dis-ease that arose with each new indication that her brain's neural connections were synchronizing with another. I chose to focus instead on the reassuring way she spoke of him as a kind of man-tool assisting her experiments and regularly pointing out how little they had in common outside of the bedroom.

I was so successful at focusing on what she was saying rather than how she was acting that I was blindsided the first time she decided she wanted him to pick her up at the airport. I was stunned both by her decision and the thoughtless way she told me—via email less than 24 hours before she was supposed to land. A week earlier I'd booked a babysitter, cleared my work day, and happily rearranged my obligations because airport retrieval was sacred time—the tweener space between travel and home, fertile for reflection, insight, and intimacy. It felt like an earned privilege, and now, she was just handing that privilege to him. *How can the mere ownership of a single anatomical organ hold equal currency to two years of our kind of intimacy?*

To mitigate the hurt, I did some impressive mental gymnastics to skip the brewing disappointment at being dumped from my role as first greeter, and pivoted towards the line of her email in which she suggested that we spend the day together upon her return. *See, the fact that she wants him to pick her up is just another experiment. She's still making our time together a priority. There's no need to be jealous.*

That next morning I was up at 5:00 AM buzzing with anticipation for that first hug, my arms practically aching for the familiar feeling. Knowing she'd been home just minutes away all night made me feel like a kid on Christmas waiting for the household to wake so we could open presents. When Naomi texted at 7:00 AM I was giddy.

NAOMI 7:08: Did you see the sunrise?

KRISTEN 7:08: Yes! Amazing.

NAOMI 7:09: See you soon. xo

See, even in bed with him, we're still connected.

The sitter arrived at 9:55 sharp. I slipped out the front door and sat on my front stoop, riveted by the ticking down of the final two minutes on the screen of my cell phone. 9:58... 9:59... 10:00! I punched 'send' on my text—*On my way!*—and peeled out of the driveway. I hastily parked and then skip-ran down the curvy path from the street towards Naomi's house before I pushed through the fence door—and stopped dead in my tracks. His truck was parked along the far side of her house. My heart dropped like a stone into my stomach.

KRISTEN 10:02: Are you there?

No response.

KRISTEN 10:04: I'm at the front door.

At 10:05 I called her, but there was no answer. I felt nauseous. *What are my options here?* Hesitantly, I knocked on door. Lightly at first, then more firmly so she might hear me in the back bedroom.

Nothing. The thought of pushing further in uninvited made my stomach roll. But I didn't know what else to do. I reluctantly cracked the front door just wide enough to call into the quiet house. "Naomi?"

His jeans lay crumpled on the floor just inside the dim apartment. My breath caught as though I'd been sucker punched. Until now the sex had been heady abstract theory, the other party merely a loosely sketched caricature of a man, the parameters of the experiment clean, separate from our life, together. But he was here. Right now. A real person. Naked. In her bed. Holding her. With her in a way I wasn't. Intimate in a way I couldn't know. Physical. Visceral. Sexual. Tender. Vulnerable.

From the back bedroom Naomi called out a strangled sounding, "Kristen!?"

And now he was taking my time, my intimacy, as though he were entitled to it. And she was letting him.

"Yeah." I dropped my eyes. Embarrassed. Ashamed. For her. For me.

"I need a few minutes."

"Okay." I closed the door and retreated towards the orchard to perch on the wooden fence there. My exultant excitement of minutes ago had vanished. Reality was pushing its way in, and with it, panic. Rejection. The dam in my mind was breaking, flooding me with all of the ways I'd watched her shifting in the past months, her attentions, her tastes, her time...

NAOMI 10:09: He's just leaving. Can't wait to see you!

...her language, her rhythms, her priorities...

KRISTEN 10:10: Okay. I'm waiting outside.

...distracted from her drive for greater meaning, her search for God, all the things that had brought us together, cues that I'd had to work so hard to explain away. *I'm losing her. She'd rather bed him than be with me. I can't compete.*

10:11. The part of me that had suspected something more threatening at play than mere inconsiderate flakiness forced itself front and center. The airport pick up. I couldn't shake the feeling that she had knowingly lied to me. That she'd been planning to have him pick her up even while we'd been making arrangements a week earlier. She'd never lied to me.

10:12. The memory of the day she'd literally exclaimed, "You know... I've *never* lied to you!" stunned and pride played in my head. It had felt like an acknowledgement of how different our partnership was for her. How special. The agreement was to show up open and transparent with all parts of ourselves, even the unpleasant ones. Even the hard ones. The thought that she might have knowingly hidden something from me... I could barely complete the thought.

10:14. It meant the very foundation of our relationship was being dismantled. *And she would abandon everything we have together just because he is a man, and I am not!?* I felt fury and frustration rise up in response to my utter confusion at the injustice of it all. *By mere virtue of the organ swinging between his legs, he has the magic key that allows him to touch her, engage her, know her in an arena our relationship can't cover.*

10:16. *We've known all of each other—emotionally, spiritually, practically—but part of her is behind a curtain now, hidden and inaccessible.* I despaired at the impossible unfairness that I should be told I had to sit back and watch the one person I was certain knew me, cared for me, the one person with whom I was most myself fade away. *I can't accept that—there must be a way to fix this!*

10:17. I had a vision of her standing with her arms around him, both of them looking at me with pity in their eyes. I was seized by the desire to flee, to run through the orchard, away from the embarrassment and shame. My muscles twitched with it.

10:18. Building tears burned hot just behind my eyes. I swallowed them back. I didn't want to look like I'd been crying. She could call me in any minute.

10:20. I wondered if they'd decided to go another round, and she'd simply forgotten about me sitting there on the fence. Time had warped, compressed and expanded as I'd run the gambit of emotions. I felt drained, and my thoughts turned fatalistic. Coldly self-loathing.

Pathetic. Only a pathetic person waits for someone that would rather be with someone else.

10:22. By the time I heard his truck pulling around, I was broken. I mustered a polite half wave as he drove by and dropped off the fence, feet landing heavily on the ground. So strong was the urge to collapse that I had to jam my hands in my pockets, elbows locked and shoulders hiked up to keep myself propped upright, to plod the fifty yards back to Naomi's door. She threw it open with a bright, "Hiiiii, friiiiend!" but something flashed subtly across her face. I could see the gears of her mind turn nimbly as she took in my expression and posture.

My response came out a froggy half whisper, "You know, if you wanted to be with him—"

"No-oo! I wanted him to get out of here so we could get started! I'm so happy to see you!" She threw her arms around me, but I only became more brittle at her touch. She began offering up chipper explanations, "He was doing the dishes, but he was sooo slow I finally had to just tell him to leave—" I took in her words with a detached analysis, some part of me repelled by the way her cheery intonations clashed discordantly with my recent thoughts. "—Our phones weren't in the bedroom, and we thought it was only 9:00—" She busily pried my hands out of my pockets and continued to lightly serve up justifications. "—but then I heard you and realized it must already be 10:00!" She tugged my arms toward her and placed them at her waist. I saw them rather than felt them there, unyielding, in a scarecrow's pantomime of a hug. They seemed to have forgotten how excited they'd been to hold her, to mold themselves to the familiar small of her back. "—I'd turned the ringer off, so I didn't hear your texts—" My mind, like my arms, felt numb. I was both clutching to the hope that we were still fine, that I hadn't lost my person, and I was gripped by the fear that she might be lying right now.

In the face of her chatter, my juxtaposed silence only grew louder until it permeated the space. Naomi finally fell quiet in surrender to it. She put her head on my shoulder, drew her full body against mine more tightly, and waited.

"I feel so stupid." Naomi's heavy outbreath felt the only appropriate response. "I was so excited to see you." My words emerged slowly. Thick. Deliberate. "I woke up this morning happy. I could barely wait for 10:00 to come... I missed seeing you so much last night. But it was going to be okay because we had this time set aside today to be together. Now I feel like a fool—" emotion clogged my throat even as I remained resolute, "—because you cared so little that you couldn't even be bothered to set a fucking alarm."

Naomi's head snapped up sharply at my language. My gaze remained stiffly focused beyond her. "I don't know what to do." Tears flowed freely down my face, and I did nothing to stop them. "I am the less desired partner." She let out a pitiful groan and fully reengaged her embrace, burying her head in my neck. I shook my head, at a loss. "I just don't know what to do."

With the weight of my truth released, life began to flow back in and replace the numbness. I entwined my fingers at the small of her back and tucked my chin into the crook of her collarbone. There were no words left. We held the weight of one another knowing that I'd thrown down all my cards, there was no game to be won here, no strategy to be played, just my confusion and hope and pain at the threat of losing us and the risk that came with such naked admittance. I was at her mercy. I was vulnerable. And I was free of pretending it was otherwise.

Data Analysis:

There's a concept in neurobiology called brain coupling. It is the means by which we are able to understand one another—the more synced two peoples' brains become, the better they are at communicating concepts to each other. There was a fascinating study done to track this brain coupling in which one person told the story of going to their high school prom while a second person listened. Scientist watched the subjects' brainwaves and found that when the partners were strangers brain wave readouts showed, as expected, a minor lag from storyteller to listener. Also expected, readings of well-acquainted pairings showed near synchronicity. What is most astounding about this study, however, is the third set of parings, those subjects who were in such intimate relationship with one another that the listener's brain waves were *ahead* of the storyteller's. Without knowing the narrative, these listeners' brains were coupled so strongly that they were actually *accurately anticipating* coming communication.

Naomi and I had been like that. We had been able to communicate without words. Our concepts of intimacy resonated with one another, our relationship based on our mutual agreement to show up with one another totally, to allow the other to know us completely. We had even named it the Friendship Lab, and I reveled in the luck at being one half of it.

It's not like we all haven't experienced a friend disappearing into new relationship before. Friend is social, friend gets boyfriend, friend disappears for a few months. It's disappointingly cliché. But I'd never before experienced such complete resonance with another brain. The tuning fork of my being had lifted amidst the harmonies of our friendship. It was as though I'd been gifted heightened energy, life force, emotion, and self-knowledge that couldn't be accessed on my own. I desired more, to uncover wholly new languages of resonance. And now, here a new note had opened up within my partner, but it was tuned to another. Its waves were crashing discordantly into our harmonies.

I feared this sexual resonance might be her keynote. I feared that where it aligned, the rest of her might follow.

Conclusion:

Intimacy comes in many forms; resonance between two people can strike between minds, bodies, or souls. If you need proof of this, just look at the myriad of extramarital relationships that can spur jealousy and insecurity. Sexual, yes, but emotional connection, intellectual sparring, a cohort in creative synchronization, strangers with shared experiences or pasts, mirrored curiosities about the world, common interests in activities as benign as biking or birdwatching—the mind of a threatened partner can conjure up innumerable iterations.

We live in a time of sexual spectrums and gender fluidity, but the way our culture recognizes partnership is still, in many ways, antiquated. Does sexual intimacy alone make a primary partnership? Emotional intimacy? Is our Primary determined by who strikes a chord with our most essential resonance, or is it a matter of which human holds a critical mass of our full range? At this moment of flux, we have the opportunity to begin investigating these questions.

Just because we live in a time in which we *can* be in any intimate partnership we choose doesn't mean there's not still an innate internal alignment that happens to be the most fulfilling for each of us individually. This isn't about turning our intimate realms into *The Lord of the Flies* or throwing our most tender feelings to the wolves. Certainly, we are free to experiment for experimentation's sake. But perhaps the more interesting thread to follow is experimentation in pursuit of discovering our deepest, most satisfying innate alignment. Rather than feel the need to sample every dessert on the seemingly endless buffet of relationship options, we have the chance to honestly own our particular needs and desires within a particular relationship and go about building that.

Delving into this new frontier is about becoming vigilant in our self-awareness, communicating our notes to another and listening to theirs in turn. It's about taking on a new intensity of discernment. We have to step up to a whole new level of parenting for our love-heart to make sure she is cared for and protected, that we are moving into gentle, kind, correct relationships with the intention of nurturing her, helping her grow and thrive. With great freedom comes great responsibility.

If we accept that role and undertake this play together, our skills of communicating intention take on paramount importance. When things were 'simple' eons ago, everyone's intentions were clearly dictated by societal norms, and the opportunities for misunderstanding were limited. Now that the lock's been taken off the cage, as it were, we have more responsibility for our own boundary setting, clarifying of expectations, desires, and non-desires. It's knowing that when everything is available on the menu, we have to be that much more specific in articulating precisely what we want.

Rest assured that our tones of resonance shift and change, so if we continue to observe, be honest about what feels important in the moment, and take the next step with the information available, no friendship, partnership, or Primary will ever feel stale. It's up to each of us to uncover and communicate our signature cocktail of intimacy resonance.

Run Your Own Experiment No. 11:

The purpose of this experiment is to amplify our awareness of how many resonances with which we align so that we can observe those already being met and those we'd like to consciously tune within partnership.

Experimental Procedure:

1. On a piece of paper, list three relationships in which you feel close to another person.

2. Next to each name, write out the areas you feel in sync with them. Be as specific as possible. (Ex. *easy conversation, same reading interests, matched intellectually, sexually compatible, amazing hug buddy, comparable relationship with God, similar childhoods, backgrounds, struggles, successes, etc.*)

3. Are there any areas of intimacy synchronicity you've enjoyed in the past or wish you could enjoy that are not currently on the list? Write down those as well.

4. On a separate sheet of paper, list the areas of intimacy you've identified in the order of most to least important. If you find

your mind quibbling and arguing, drop into your body and simply go with your gut response.

5. How many of these do you require your primary partner to satisfy? Only your number one? Your top three? Six of your top ten? Draw a line under the number you land on.

Bonus Steps:

1. If you are currently in a recognized Primary relationship— friendship, romantic, work wife, whatever—consider whether he or she meets your desired intimacies.

   a. If yes, set the time to acknowledge and speak them aloud with your Primary.

   b. If not, write out why you feel comfortable making an exception for them.

2. If you currently do not have a recognized Primary,

   a. Consider whether there is a relationship you are currently in that is meeting many or all of your important resonances.

   b. If there is, take note. If not, keep this list in mind as you engage prospective partners going forward.

CHAPTER TWELVE
Publish Your Findings

pub·lish /ˈpəbliSH/:
to print (a finding) in a book or journal so as to make it generally known; to make a public announcement of; to disseminate to the public; to announce formally or officially; proclaim; promulgate

SUBJECT: Overthinker; Female; Age 31 years, 9 months, 27 days.

HYPOTHESIS: Achieving primary resonance, and thus, Primary Partnership establishes mutual implied commitment.

METHOD: Rene Zellweger, ring shopping, Joni Mitchell.

FIELD SITE: Naomi's cozy kitchen table.

Experiment 151.22.0:

I'm in love with Naomi. Beat. My hands flew up to my mouth, covering the stunned smile that had broken out. *Holy cow! I'm in love with Naomi!* I repeated the words over and over again in my head, charged by my abrupt discovery, luxuriating in my newfound membership to a privileged group. *I'm in love with Naomi.*

It wasn't enough to say it to myself. I had to say it aloud. I had to tell someone. I called my brother in New York. It was after ten there. He was a twenty-something in the theatre scene. There was no way he was going to pick up. But he was the person I wanted to tell. He was the person who would hear me. I was planning the message I was going to leave on his voicemail when he answered. "Hey."

"Hey! Hi. Do you have a minute?"

"Yeah. What's going on?"

"I just—I have to say something—aloud—" I was tripping over my words, buzzing with nervous excited energy, on the verge of unleashing something into the world that would forever change things. A confession or a declaration, I wasn't sure, but all of my thoughts and feelings were trying to push their way out at once. "I've just realized, I'm in love with Naomi."

"Oh, wow." The two syllables carried every ounce of gravity and understanding I'd hoped they would.

"I know. I *know!*" I'd said it aloud. I couldn't believe I'd said those words aloud! I covered my face and grinned, dancing around the living room, full of jittery adrenaline. "I just—she's been on this solo retreat, she was planning to be in silence for seven days which would have ended tomorrow, but then my phone rang, and it was her name, and I was *so* excited, and she said, 'I wanted yours to be the first voice I heard,' and it just made me happier than I'd ever been! And we talked, and when I hung up I just couldn't stop smiling, I mean, I literally couldn't. It was so strange, but something about it felt familiar too, and I suddenly recognized it—I was behaving like Renee Zellweger or Ann Hathaway or the way that all of those women behave in romantic comedies. It's that *thing*. And it came at me like a ton of bricks: I was behaving like a girl in love! And I know it looks nothing like it's supposed to. I think that's why I missed it for so long, but there's no denying it. I am. I'm in love with Naomi."

Naomi had left on a solo retreat not long after my confession of feeling like the less desired partner. She was still in her sexual study to be sure, but I'd been restored to my position as her closest confidant. She'd reassured me that the guy wasn't a threat, confided that he'd become clingy, too relationship-y. She told me he'd started to indicate that he wanted more than just sex. We'd laughed together at the thought of her holding hands while strolling publicly through the Sunday farmer's market with a *boyfriend.* "Ugh!" The image had made her visibly cringe. "I'm going to tell him we need to take the holidays off. I need some space." By the end I almost couldn't believe I'd been worried about this caricature of a man taking my place.

I realized I was in love with her a few weeks before Christmas. Unlike my shift from *virgin* to *girl who's had sex,* my state of change from *never been in love* to *in love* was palpable. The secret knowledge of my new, forever-changed-self fed me and filled me with joy at spontaneous moments throughout the day. I left for Christmas vacation happy that Naomi was at last emerging from the sex fog of the past three months. She seemed to be returning to the land of functional reasoning, again able to make and follow through with conscious decisions rather than simply living at the mercy of a man's call. The woman I'd spent my life with these past years, my partner in both the search for the cutest new yoga pants and the meaning of life, the woman I'd *fallen in love with,* was returning.

During the two weeks I was away, I found myself lingering at jewelry stands. Naomi's words months earlier about an imagined ceremony rang in my ears, and I wondered how she might respond if I returned with matching gold rings for us. I began to playfully refer to the vacation she and I had planned for June as our honeymoon. I couldn't wait to get back to see her.

"I told him I loved him."

I froze. "What? You...you, what?"

"We ended up spending the entire holiday together."

"But when I left you said you wanted time ... that he was going to be with his family."

"I know, but he came over, and he'd gotten me a gift, this ridiculous shirt just like the ones he wears, and I had gotten him a few things, and then he just, kind of ... stayed. And we holed up here all Christmas. And I just, I felt the impulse to do it, and I told him I love him."

What is happening? I had not seen this coming. The way she'd talked about him to me—like their sexual dalliance had an inevitable expiration date—had it all been a lie? Was our continued future-planning just her management of my feelings? Or had my wishful thinking kept me willfully blind?

"And you know what gave me the strength to tell him?" I shook my head. Naomi's tone turned almost shy. "That day you came down here and told me you felt like the less loved partner. You were just so honest. So vulnerable. It inspired me." I blinked. She seemed to think this confession bestowed a coveted honorific rather than a mortal blow.

"So, are you ... what are you? Dating?"

"I don't know. I mean, no, it's not like I'm going to *tell* anyone about him."

"Oh." I felt a spark of hope. For anyone else this would be an odd thing to say, but I'd seen her do this with so many friends and acquaintances; she'd keep each relationship cloaked within her intensely private world; separate from the rest of her life and from one another. If she was leaving herself an out, keeping things clean and under her control; if she didn't love him in a way that made her climb to the top of the clock tower and claim their relationship to the world then maybe this was just another experiment. Maybe this was her trying on being in love the way she'd been trying out sexual escapades. Maybe I hadn't lost her yet. Maybe I still had a chance.

I needed to tell Naomi that I was in love with her, that I didn't want her to leave what we had, that I did want to claim our relationship by shouting it from the clock tower. For the next three weeks I knew I had to tell her, but I was terrified. As long as I said nothing, I could hope that she wanted the same. The stakes felt impossibly high. Acknowledging I was in love would mean acknowledging how much I had to lose. Too much. Everything. Myself. But I also knew I couldn't let fear pin me down and force me to watch her walk out the proverbial door. I couldn't let our partnership just fade away.

I looked for an opening. How do you start a conversation like that? And finding the right moment was made all the more difficult by the fact that she was now earmarking all of her free time to be with him. No more were our morning walks, she was too tired from having adopted his late to bed, late to rise schedule. The recipes she'd once cooked for me were now fully reformulated to fit his tastes. Even asking her to show up to our office on time had become a point of contention because it meant cutting morning sex and his rambling stories over coffee short.

My teacher Ravi says that freedom is not, as so many of us believe, unlimited choice, but rather the *absence* of choice. True freedom is experienced when we know what we *must* do or say, when we have no choice but to act on it. She was single handedly dismembering my primary partnership, my job, and even my ability to live in peace in my own home—my life—without so much as an acknowledgement. The fire sale on our relationship hit such speeds that I finally felt there was nothing left to lose. If I did nothing, I would lose my partner. If I told her what I wanted for us, there was a chance of saving what we had. I prayed for an opportunity to arise naturally, and by the grace of God, it did. I knew it was the moment because when I checked in with myself, the fear had dissolved, and the clear, calm words I needed to say were right there waiting for me.

She'd made us breakfast, a rarity now. He'd had an early job up North. The tempting smells of ginger and onions wafted up from the plates she had just set on the table, but even her cooking couldn't hold my attention in the moment. Sitting across the tiny table from her, our calves rested against one another in the kind of casual entanglement of limbs to which we were accustomed. The words that had been formulating for the last two months chose this quiet, ordinary moment to be born.

"I miss you. I want our partnership back. I want us to be committed to being there for one another, caring for one another. I'm...You know, I'm just...so in love with you. I want to be with you. I want us to be together the way we have been. These have been the happiest years of my life. I want us to spend our days together. I want to be there for you when you're excited or sick or sad. I want to be the one who gets to hold you when you cry. I want to be the one to comfort you. And I want to have a language of physical intimacy. I want to be free to reach over and touch you. I want it to be okay for us to hang out skin to skin while we're watching a movie. I want to be your partner in the work of living all the aspects of this life. I don't want to lose us. That's what I want."

The monologue flowed out of me unapologetically. I felt no fear, I did not fumble my words, I did not have to push myself through it. I was in love with Naomi. I'd had no choice but to tell her. And Ravi had been right, I felt free.

Data Analysis:

There's a reason Joni Mitchell's "Big Yellow Taxi" has been covered as many times as it has. It seems to be a universal law of the human condition that "you don't know what you've got 'till it's gone." There's something about the real threat of loss that clarifies things, that allows us to see the one and only option ahead of us. And that focus of energy gives us access to decision-making, action, strength, and outright bravery to fight for it. Feeling your back against a wall reveals the surprising truth of what's happening. In my case, I was shocked to find that I was ready to claim commitment.

When I fell in love with Naomi, I was surprised to find 'traditional' urges begin to spontaneously arise within me. Thoughts of rings and vows emerged unbidden. Images of proclaiming our commitment in front of friends danced through my mind. I viscerally wanted to publicly claim and be claimed by the woman before me. To me, the titles, rights, and recognition of primary partnership, the traditions and signifiers of commitment truly felt, for the first time in my life, like freedom.

You see, until that moment I'd been, like so many of us in these modern times, mistaking the word 'commitment' for 'confinement.' We've done a funny thing to commitment in the last generation or two. We've collectively put off the age of marriage even as we continue to seek companionship, thereby creating a commitment tweener zone. In the 1950s when the median age of marriage was twenty (women) and twenty-two (men) years old, the act of dating had a clear purpose: to find a life mate. Seventy-five percent of women were getting married by their early twenties at that time, so one can imagine that a sixteen-year-old girl looked towards the next four to six years of dating as a finite stage of life with a focused purpose.

Now a-days we've extended the median age for that first marriage by seven years. This amidst a culture-wide drop in the percentage of people getting married at all. As a result, our dating lifespans can cover ten, fifteen, twenty-plus years! In this new landscape the 'why' of dating has become less clear.

With marriage no longer the assumed end game, there are a myriad of intentions and unendingly nuanced types of commitment a person might seek (and, therefore, unending opportunity for misalignments and misunderstandings). Many of us are on vigilant lookout for someone we'll like *just enough* that we enjoy spending time with them, but not *so* much that we accidentally find ourselves compelled to commit to them. How many of us have uttered the words, "I mean, it's not that I don't want to settle down someday, I'm just not ready to yet." For years or decades we busily search out not-quite-right matches to protect ourselves from falling victim to the spontaneous and unplanned compulsion to build a nurturing and sustainable life with someone.

I hadn't realized that I'd been unconsciously convinced that my life was a black and white choice between committed partnership and personal freedom. Falling in love with Naomi woke me up to the fact that these two states weren't actually in opposition. I found myself compelled to claim what we meant to one another aloud, to articulate the ways we wanted to be there for one another, to speak of the agreement we'd already been functionally living out and talking around for years specifically *because* our partnership was energizing, empowering, strengthening to me as an individual. Because her presence made me feel like I could do more in the world, not less. I wanted us to hear one another proclaim aloud the commitment we were already living by, the promise to be there with one another through every challenge and every inevitable change and find a way to integrate all the newness into the relationship. I wanted our friends and families and strangers to recognize and honor this commitment, and in recognizing this innate desire in myself, I could understand, finally, the error of my thinking. Freedom doesn't exist in the absence of commitment. Commitment is freedom.

Conclusion:

There is no relationship without commitment. I mean it. It is literally impossible for a relationship to exist without it. Commitment is the sturdy framework that holds space for the chaotic mess of two people showing up as themselves and bouncing into one another in an experiment of resonance. Some of these experiments succeed in varying degrees of synchronicity, and others outright fail, but without commitment the chance of human connection is a null set.

Still uncomfortable with the word? Let's take it out of the realm of romance for a moment, then. All of our well-functioning, satisfying relationships require a commitment between two people. This is true within all relationship constructs.

» Co-workers: I commit to do my best, to do what you need me to do by the deadline we've agreed to.

» Therapeutic relationships: I commit to be here for one hour every Tuesday and let you show up as whoever you are that day without judgement.

» Your local barista: I commit to have coffee hot and on hand between the hours of 6:00 AM and 8:00 PM daily.

» Your postal carrier: I commit to not forget your packages in the back of my truck for three days and chuck them on your doorstep crushed, mangled, and covered with unidentifiable stains.

» Friendships: I commit to pick up your calls, show up for our lunch dates no more than fifteen minutes late, hate your boyfriend when you hate him and say wonderful things about him when you make up.

There are many commitments in our lives that are surface, and appropriately so. My hairdresser and I do not have a lifelong commitment to not go to bed angry nor laugh at one another's jokes. (In fact, her commitment to me is to let me sit there in blessed silence and read for a whole hour.) There are those rare relationships, however—and these are once in a blue moon—that encompass a commitment so vast as to be held in a single sentence: We commit to be in relationship by working through and incorporate our individual needs now and when they inevitably change. (If you find someone able to enter that commitment with you, run to them. *Run to them!*)

Lest you think I'm still pointing towards an antiquated concept, realize that even the commitment to be uncommitted is a mutual promise, an agreed upon intention. It's a commitment to not let jealousy get the best of you, to tell your partner honestly about the moments that it does, to reassess together in a constructive and caring manner when circumstances and feelings shift and change and result in different rates of change in different areas of the internal landscape. Honestly, commitment to a successful non-committed relationship might require the most rigorous commitment of all.

I don't know that commitment needs to be forever for it to be freeing, most contracts we enter have specified expiration dates for a reason. Nor do I believe that our definition of satisfying commitment remains static throughout our lives. Perhaps precisely because of this, there is value in speaking in a commitment language in matters of love, in consciously recognizing the millions of little expectations and promises that make up a relationship, whatever form it may take. Publishing, verbalizing, our commitments to one another or to the world gives them a clarity they don't otherwise hold. Be it as simple as committing to show up for a date next week or as nuanced as laying out the expectations in your gender-fluid polyamorous marriage, speaking the agreement between you and your partner builds a sturdy foundation for whatever playground you've committed to explore together.

Claim commitment for yourself. Claim the freedom.

Run Your Own Experiment No. 12:

The purpose of this identify our established relational agreements so we can consciously move into future commitments.

Experimental Procedure:

1. Consider the relationship you consider primary in your life.

2. On a piece of paper, write out all of the specific commitments that make up your relationship with this person. You might consider these categories:

    a. Overarching formal commitments *(Ex. he commits to our marriage, she commits to work while I raise the children, she commits to not bring her other partners to our home)*

    b. Emotional commitments *(Ex. she commits to not be cruel, he to never call me out when I'm behaving like my mother)*

    c. Practical daily-life commitments *(Ex. she takes out the garbage, he does the bills, he keeps my favorite coffee stocked, she gives me a break from the kids for an hour after getting home from work)*

3. Review your list and put a star next to all of the commitments that have been spoken aloud within the relationship.

4. Circle those which are silent agreements. Consider acknowledging these unspoken commitments to your partner today with grateful intention.

Bonus Steps:

1. Consider a relationship that is currently disappointing you.

2. On a piece of paper, write down all of the ways this disappointment is manifesting.

3. *(i.e. what are the commitments you and the other person are breaking?)*

4. Circle those which are unspoken.

5. Bring up these circled items within your relationship, and discover whether your partner was aware that you consider them commitments. Likewise, investigate whether your partner might presume unspoken commitments of which you are unaware.

PART III

Data
Analyisis

CHAPTER THIRTEEN

Enlist Assistant Data Analysts

a·nal·y·sis /əˈnaləsəs/:
a process of inspecting, cleansing, transforming, and modeling data with the goal of discovering useful information, suggesting conclusions, and supporting decision-making

SUBJECT: Overthinker; Female; Age 31 years, 10 months.

HYPOTHESIS: Because I am both subject and scientist, any attempts I make to analyze the data of previous relationship experiments are suspect. An unbiased third party from outside of the experimental construct is required if I am to uncover any useful conclusions.

METHOD: Archetypes, denial, neurobiology.

FIELD SITE: A softly lit, cream-colored twelve by fifteen foot room.

Experiment 160.21.5:

"And what of Aphrodite?"

I cocked my head at Dr. Sparrow. I could hear the devil's advocate dancing behind her mild-mannered way. I shot her a sly smile, up for the game. "What *of* Aphrodite?"

She loved a good archetype, and I enjoyed batting them around in her cozy office. There was something reassuring in discovering that my experiences might merely be confirming data of the universal workings of humanity as captured in ancient stories of the gods. It made me feel less weird. "Well, she's a goddess. Of sexual desire. And when you turn your back on a goddess—"

"That's just it!" I interrupted, "Have I turned my back on her? Or are we just in a fist-bump, 'hey guuurl,' casual kind of relationship?" Although my delivery was playful Dr. Sparrow heard the earnestness in my question and gave me her full attention. "I've been researching the chemicals the brain releases in the course of sex. A lot of what came up, of course, were these, 'You too can have one-night stands like a man!' 'Be not a slave to your hormones!' articles. You know, *Cosmo Magazine* kind of pieces rather than scientific studies.

I continued, "I found it interesting, though, that even *these* articles, in the course of championing the one-night stand, made a point of the fact that the behavior they were advising was <u>not</u> the doorway into a loving, sustainable partnership. They acknowledge that long-term relationship requires a deliberate building of trust with another in a way that can only be cultivated over time. Obviously, we know that sex can make us feel like we have those long-term things—that total trust with someone—even when we don't. But is sex *required* for partnership? I have to believe it's possible to come to that kind of loving partnership through building trust and vulnerability outside of the bedroom.

"From what I understand, or from what I've heard from couples who have been married for some time, sex becomes less the thing as time goes on. Or it becomes one single tool in a whole toolbox of ways to maintain and strengthen an existing relationship. Those partnerships become more about the other types of closeness and intimacy—the emotional, spiritual, practical ways of being together, right? So, why can't a relationship *start* there?

"No, I've not had the kneejerk biological desire to have sex, but I've had *that*. I've had the vulnerability, the devotion, the total trust of a loving partnership. So, I have to question what Aphrodite means by 'sexual desire.' I've never felt compelled to the act of sex with someone out of chemical lust, but I *have* been overcome by desire—for intimacies of trust, of mutual vulnerability. I've lusted for additional methods and languages by which to express the connection of our hearts, the synced-up state of our brains, the soul link that is beyond my ability to put into words. And I've felt compelled to create with someone, to birth ideas with, to bring a shared future to term with another.

"Look," I leveled with her, "when you and I have spoken of my relationship with Naomi in here, we've had to use romantic language. There's just been no other option, no other way to talk about it. And when you and I speak of the end of my relationship with Naomi, we talk about it as a divorce. We use terms of devastation and loss and jealousy and heartbreak. Am I really to believe that Aphrodite would not accept this offering of heart and soul over the technicality of never having attempted physical orgasm together?"

I shifted forward, practically leaning off the couch towards Dr. Sparrow as though being in closer proximity might make her more fully understand my meaning. "My whole life I've observed how sex can trigger the brain into thinking we're in love, how it hooks people and leads them blindly down a path into attachments in which they sacrifice their identities and give their desires and dreams over completely to a person who was careless with these gifts. I wanted no part of that. Since I seemed to be missing that hormonal thing that made people want to have sex on sight, I figured I was safe. But look at me." I raised my hands, palms up in supplication. "I never slept with Naomi, and still I was caught by eros. I was held by desire and ready to offer my life over completely as fodder for *our* life." I shook my head and slumped back against the couch before looking Dr. Sparrow square in the eye. "You tell me where I've been these past years if not the realm of Aphrodite."

Naomi told me 'no' four days after I confessed I wanted a recognized partnership. When she told me, she said she'd wished it could be a different answer, tried to make it a different answer, wondered why it couldn't be a different answer, but it was a no. Her dharma was to be played out with a man.

I did an admirable job of holding respectful space for her to share this, graciously accepted her answer as her truth. Once she unburdened we spoke brightly about the fact that, yet again, we'd headed fearlessly towards the unexplored fringes of defined relationship and showed up bravely and honestly with one another. I walked away from the conversation proud of us. Another day of good work in Friendship Lab.

In many ways things continued as they had. Daily we sat side by side in our small office. We still lived a stone's throw from one another. We talked and texted in the few spaces where she wasn't now otherwise occupied with her new primary partner. We still planned to travel together over my birthday in April, and the vacation I'd previously thought of as our honeymoon was still on the books, though baring different nomenclature.

But things continued to shift. As her mirror neurons aligned ever more rapidly with alien resonances, we fell ever more out of cellular sync. I had a front row seat to watch the one person on the planet who I felt truly saw me fade before my very eyes. I desperately fought within myself to stave off the injustice of it all. I soldiered on incessantly, insistently hopeful, determined to find the best logical plan, the most workable new iteration of 'us' in the face of what might otherwise be felt as crushing loss. To do anything else would have been to give up the relationship entirely, and that was inconceivable.

My logic brain was certain we could find a way to be friends, but my physical body was unconvinced. Every time I heard his truck, each individual nerve ending painfully pricked with adrenaline as if urgently alerting me to a threat. A rush of panicked blood pumped through every time she was late coming into work. Each small withdrawal of her attention and love was torture, a chasm of rejection followed by the threat of crippling depression at each small abandonment of what we'd had—each abandonment of me.

At times, the fury, the jealousy, the thrashing desperation that took hold of me was disturbingly animalistic. I worked hard to rise above the emotional tumult, to bypass the angry images of self-defense and revenge that hijacked my imagination without warning. My body and brain were being torn apart by the dissonance between logic and feeling. *Everything's fine, your friend just got a boyfriend* butted up against the certainty of *We are being slowly flayed alive!!!* The sheer intensity was intolerable. I felt crazy. Unable to control my inner world. I was under siege, and the one person I could count on to calm me was the very source of my pain.

I could turn to no one else because I didn't know how to talk about it. I had no *right* to any of these reactions because there was no recognized partnership. Naomi was, after all, neither my lover nor wife. Whatever we were to one another, our partnership had never been declared with any formality nor recognized publicly as a commitment. Rather, I'd experienced everyday declarations in every little decision, each conscious inter-winding, the countless I love you's. Had we slept together I could at least have pointed to that benchmark of validation, but in the absence of this one logistical piece there was no couples therapy, no family encouraging us to work it out. There was no friend with a pint of ice cream. There's was no permissiveness or understanding that some days I had to fight to get out from under the covers because lying in bed until I faded away seemed the preferable option to getting up and going through my day without her love and attention.

And any thought I did have to reach out to someone was halted by visions of raised eyebrows, the implication in their expressions that I must be hiding something, that for me to be this broken there must be something illicit going on here, I must be lying about the nature of our relationship. I would look crazy and obsessive. The crushing blow of being so misunderstood was too much of a risk.

For two weeks after she gave me her 'no,' I was under the impression that I was doing a decent job of holding it together. I wasn't so sure after the nervous breakdown. It was the day after Valentine's Day (a detail I didn't note until much later). Alone in our office, my phone dinged with a text from her.

Naomi: I've realized I need to take a break from people.

I froze. Is she talking about me? *She must be talking about me. She's thought it over and decided she thinks I'm a problem, and she's cutting me out...right?* I tried to keep my desperation out of my response.

Me: Oh yeah? Any particular people?

The screen stayed blank. No response. I watched the second hand ticking by on the clock. One minute. Two minutes. Three minutes. *This is it. It's already done. She's gone. I screwed up. I did it wrong. She's cut me out like Amanda did. It's happened again.* I collapsed to the floor. I was conscious, but blank. All thoughts had left my mind. I became a blinking cursor on a clean page.

It might have been a relief. Had I been capable of feeling relief. Looking back, I've wondered whether it was my built-in failsafe, a reboot of the system that kicked in when the circuits got dangerously hot. I suppose it was what I'd always suspected about falling in love— my emotion chip had overwhelmed my neural net.

It could have been funny. Had I been able to find things funny. I'd thought I was safe from this because I didn't desire a husband, didn't feel a hormone driven craving for sex. But love had snuck in a side door. It had come dressed in a disguise that looked so unlike anything I could have recognized as romantic partnership that it hadn't tripped my radar. And now, here I was, drowning in it, illogical and irrationally broken.

I considered none of these things in my blank state.

Shadows marched across my body at angles and crept up the far wall.

The cursor in my brain remained idle. —*blink—blink—blink—*

My systems came back on line with the same lack of warning with which they had gone down. The blinking cursor began to again type thoughts through my mind. I looked up at the clock. Noon. I had lost three hours.

Still sitting on the floor of the silent office, muscle memory swiped my thumb across the screen of my phone. Earlier that morning, I'd opened *Psychology Today's* website, punched in my zip code, and, out of curiosity, scanned the pages for a friendly face. The therapist's profile I'd perused was still open on the screen. I pressed my thumb to the blue underlined phone number and brought the phone to my ear. It was a voicemail recording. I waited for the beep.

"Hi, Dr. Sparrow. My name is Kristen Smith, and—" I snapped my mouth shut and tried to capture the sob rising in my chest before the machine could. I breathed slowly into a long pause—too long a pause—trying to regain enough control to speak. When I continued, my I sounded strained and foreign, "—and I need help."

Data Analysis:

Without adequate data analysis the experimentation cycle is left incomplete. The experiment becomes impotent and purposeless. Hypotheses become mere guesses, and experimentation becomes interpretation rather than truth seeking. To experiment without drawing data-based conclusion is abuse of the scientific method.

But I was incapable of impartial analysis. Dr. Sparrow was the one to use the word 'heartbreak' in our first session. When she spoke it, I wept. The single word delivered with such matter-of-fact acknowledgement validated my entire experience. It made it real, and it's utterance by another gave me permission to use all the other words I'd not allowed myself: lovesick, partner, wife, attraction, desire, jealousy, affair, divorce. Dr. Sparrow's small office held the total volume of air in which my relationship with Naomi was fully recognized as the near marriage it had been to me. Only here could it be openly grieved.

For years, I'd waved off my affection for Naomi or given the feeling another name. I'd been unable to fit such emotions in any of the neatly sorted boxes of understanding that made up my being. But the thing's inability to be categorized, its unwillingness to lay well sorted in the curio cabinet of drawers in my chest, its insistence at bursting forth and declaring itself to me to be true blue Jane Austin butterflies and starry eyes Aphrodite sanctioned IN LOVE made little sense to me. I was in doubt of everything I'd experienced and needed an outside perspective to carry me into a previously inaccessible lexicon of expression reserved only for the most formulaic of heartbreaks. Only then did I feel confident in my conclusion of IN LOVE.

As I gained proficiency in the language reserved for lovers, my heartbreak sometimes felt so voluminous that it strained the walls of Dr. Sparrow's office. Airports became my secret refuge. They have long been one of my favorite places of anonymity. You can have entire conversations with people about the deepest parts of your life and try on different framings of your story in each encounter. The soaring ceilings and cavernous terminals provide a container large enough to hold not only all the complexity of your life but of the millions of others passing through. When a stranger would strike up a conversation I was able to engage my new lexicon.

"It's been about a year since my partner left me."

The stranger sitting next to me would offer an empathetic head dip of acknowledgement. "What happened?"

"She found someone else. That's really what it came down to. I wanted to be with her. She wanted to be with this guy. There's really no getting around that."

"How long were you together?" My layover companion cum confidant would ask before taking a draft off his beer.

"Two years. We were friends a while before that, but we were in a primary partnership two years before she left. It wouldn't be so bad, but it's just...I miss having my *person*, you know? That person who is on the same wavelength, who already is laughing about something before you've even pointed it out to them. I miss feeling like there's someone on this planet who knows me." The empathy in the stranger's face, the 'girl, I been there' head nod would feel like a breath of fresh air to a suffocating woman. In those moments it felt like I was closer to Truth.

And the effect of making these small, creeping claims on my experience was compounding. So much so that when I encountered a book called *Heartbreak*, I was able to engage it un-self-consciously. Its author Dr. Ginette Paris further reinforced the viability of the data from my experiments via the lens of neurobiology.

"Your brain reacts like that of a drug addict suddenly deprived of his/her drug, the behavior of the love-crazy is similar to that of the addict desperately searching for a fix. In your case, the 'fix' is the abandoner." (p. 60)

The science and jargon were reassuring companions to my confused and disoriented rational self.

"Your brain does not differentiate between lack of love, the lack of food, or the lack of sleep. A threat is a threat." (p. 61)

It was comforting to know that the unfamiliar and often unsettling experiences of myself were actually side effects, symptoms, signs of a biology in repair. When Naomi had pulled away from our partnership, I'd felt like Velcro being slowly ripped apart. I felt physical pain, my being full of gaping voids where she had once held space. I felt utterly alone in the experience since she, it seemed, did not have to suffer this way. Her half of the Velcro was simply being transferred to another, so she felt no void, no pain. I was left a walking open wound. And now I understood why.

"When the purveyor of love abandoned you, all the bundles of synapses that connected you to that person remained active, but with no response, creating a situation of emotional inertia. The lack of echo is experienced as the inner abyss into which you fall. When you are cut off from a partner your brain literally

has to reconfigure its connections. Until your brain is done with this updating, consider yourself handicapped: physically, emotionally, cognitively." (p. 1)

Neurobiology has become our modern version of archetype. Both point us towards the fact that fundamentally, we are all experiencing the same humanness, the same archetypical patterns as the ancients, the same firing of synapses and patterns as our survival-focused ancestors. The trickiness is that in detail our experiences can look completely unique, totally specific to our particular body and brain. Focused on those differences, we lose sight of the sameness of our existence. We can't see the universal forest for the intimate details of the tree right in front of us.

Whether you point to the strivings of the soul, survival psychology, or the organ of the brain, there is a universality to our human experience. It took outside sources to let me in on the fact that I wasn't an abomination. I was behaving like a quintessential human being in heartbreak. In fact, having the normalcy of my heartbreak revealed comforted me, that retroactively confirmed that I'd truly been in love. In fact, I can't say whether I'd ever have identified that I was in love without my heartbreak. I began to see that it had been a most precious catalyst to knowing myself. And what a reframe that was! My heartbreak was a gift.

Conclusion:

Self-experimentation is a long time-honored tradition in scientific pursuit. From Jonas Salk's offer of himself and his family as the first to receive his experimental polio vaccine to Albert Hofmann's 1943 trippy bicycle ride, those who are driven to find answers will often risk life and limb to do so. And we, the public, benefit from their bravery. But I'll put even money that when good 'ol Albert was in the middle of LSD induced hallucinations, his detached observational skills were not particularly sound.

Heartbreak is an unparalleled catalyst toward self-knowledge. "No" is nourishing. Pain is the ingredient that gets us to grow, change, get up out of our chairs and move something in our lives to be different. But we are also human with human emotions and filters of perception cobbled together imperfectly from childhood wiring. It is nearly impossible for us to remain clear-eyed while passing through the keyhole of our own trauma. Our focus upon getting to the other side, surviving the pain, correctly and necessarily tunnel-visions us. Most of us cannot see the bigger picture until we've landed safely and stretched into our new form with its new perspective.

No scientist would submit results that hadn't been reviewed by other scientists—professionals with no stake in the game, or even better, rival researchers who hope that the data will be disproven. Likewise, in our experiments in the world, we benefit from enlisting data analysts who can check our work, trace our logic, and question or confirm our conclusions. We would be just as foolish to draw universal laws—what I'll call personal truths—from within the hermetically sealed bubble of our own perspective.

The thing about approaching love and life as a series of experiments is that it is a fine dance between being scientist and lab rat. The rat cannot tell us why it runs to the cheese. We need someone to inform us when we've lost perspective. In these instances, we need others to take up the mantel of impartial observer and make rational connections to a larger trend for us. This sounding board may come in the form of friends, family, or professionals. It may be an online group or a scientific book. It might be 'bubble busters'—intentional exposure to ways of life radically different from our own in attempts to gain wider perspective of how humanity works outside of our own brains and widen our field of choices.

Regardless of method, when we are deep in the experiment it is invaluable to have a trusted data analyst along for the ride. Feedback from an impartial sounding-board helps us track the data of our experience more accurately. It holds us on a useful direction and encourages a practice of making small claims on our newly revealed reality. It drops us into a practice of finding the places where we can let our outer expression accurately reflect our inner experience. And it helps nudge us overthinkers toward our favorite thing of all: understanding.

Run Your Own Experiment No. 13:

The purpose of this experiment is to identify existing unbiased third-party resources to expand our awareness of available data analysts.

Experimental Procedure:

1. List the names of the people you reach out to when you want to hash out relationship questions or concerns. (It may be helpful to return to the list you created in Experiment No. 6 while establishing your safety protocol.)

2. On a piece of paper, write the reasons you go to this person by answering these questions:

   a. Do they mostly listen, or do they provide advice? What kind of advice?

   b. Do they counterbalance your emotions about the situation or amplify them?

   c. Do they have a stake in the outcome of your relationship?

   d. Are you trying to get anything from them by bringing your relationship problems to them?

   e. What does talking with them provide you?

   f. At the end of a conversation, do you see things differently, more broadly or clearly, or does your view remain unchallenged?

3. Considering your answers above, put a star next to those people you would consider to be suitable data analysts.

4. It is powerful to know that we have access to a reliable sounding board, and when we are at our most alone it can be easy to forget. Write this list of names somewhere where you can easily access them when you're feeling most misunderstood within your primary relationship(s). (I keep my list in my phone).

Bonus Steps

It's empowering to know we have a multitude of resources and options in front of us when we need help gaining perspective on our experience of relationship. Books, online groups, therapists, and even a well-phrased google search can connect us with diverse points of view and play devil's advocate with the voice in our heads. Take ten minutes today to do a cursory search of these resources to quantify just how much support is available when our perspective narrows to only encompass the voices in our heads.

CHAPTER FOURTEEN

Experiment Vulnerably, Experience Vulnerability

ex·per·i·ment /ikˈ-sper-ə-mənt/:
an operation or procedure carried out under controlled conditions to discover an unknown effect, test a hypothesis, or demonstrate a known fact.

ex·pe·ri·ence /ikˈ-spir-ē-ən(t)s/:
something personally encountered, undergone, or lived through; the state of having been affected by direct participation

SUBJECT: Overthinker; Female; Age 32 years, 10 months, 20 days.

HYPOTHESIS: The values of vulnerability (conducive to partnership) and self-reliance (conducive to singledom) are polar opposites, so I must choose between the two as the driving value in my life.

METHOD: Adolescent confusion, adult confrontation, abundant therapy.

FIELD SITE: Back in that same cream-colored room (it was a fruitful site).

Experiment 170.22.5:

"So, I sent an email to this woman asking her where I could book a shuttle for the trip she's organizing for us, and she responded with essentially, 'Try to figure it out yourself, and if you can't I'll look into it,' and I immediately *knew* that I'd asked one too many questions, and now in her mind I'd tipped over the line from a fun, capable person with something to offer to a helpless, needy, irritating liability."

"Just to confirm, she didn't actually say any of those things, right?"

"Oh, no, no; I'm likely making it all up. All she did was send me a one sentence reply. I know intellectually that she was probably just busy and shot off a response. But, the observable point here is that my emotional reaction was immediate despair followed by a certainty she now loathed me." I took a beat to consider, "And...you know... that still *could* be true. She *could* very well be irritated. But, no, I don't actually have any proof of that."

Dr. Sparrow's smile communicated a healthy modicum of indulgence, "Just so we're clear."

"The thing is, at the horrifying thought that this woman might now think of me as needy, I suddenly *felt* needy—*desperately* so." An involuntarily little sneer played over my lips at the memory. "It was pathetic. I never should have bothered her with something so small in the first place."

Dr. Sparrow straightened up in her chair, "Now, you know, this has come up before, this strong distaste for your needs. What is it that makes you so disapproving?"

I nodded in acknowledgement of the self-disgust that had begun coursing automatically through my limbs. "I know, I know." This wasn't new territory; I recognized where we were headed though she hadn't yet spoken the word. "My whole life I've been dogged by this *vulnerability* thing. I know it's important for relationships. I totally accept that it's something I need to embody if I want to be a fully actualized human in society. I'm one of the 30 million people who watched that Brené Brown TED Talk on the subject—do you remember how popular that thing was?—and I listen when those in the relationship now laud its powers. I get it. *Really,* I do. I'm in. I *want* to have the richest relationships I possibly can, and I do believe mutual vulnerability plays a huge part in achieving that. And, if I'm honest, I think I do a pretty decent job of it these days. You should have met me six years ago!"

"Oh?"

"Oh my gosh, you have no idea. We're in therapy 2.0 here. Back when I first walked into Dr. Patricia's office—you know, when I started seeing her after Amanda—I was a totally different person. She had her work cut out for her." I shook my head, chuckling at the memory.

Dr. Sparrow settled more deeply into her chair, encouraging me to expand, "How so?"

I let my eyes momentarily wander towards the ceiling in consideration of my entry point. *We still have forty-five minutes. What is the most useful information, and how do I share it most efficiently? What details does Sparrow need for it to allow insight? For it to be a tool for progress?* I decided to start at the beginning.

"So, growing up my dad would occasionally point out, 'Yeah, well, Kristen, you know you're not the most naturally vulnerable person.' I'd take that as an accolade even though I could hear the tinge of concern around the edges of his voice. It made me proud. I was the kid who would come to my parents with my problems only *after* I had solved them. It had always felt like an accomplishment that I could take care of myself, that I needed for no one and nothing, that I was neither bother nor burden to anyone. Being self-sufficient made me feel mature. Beholden to no one. It made me feel powerful. Like I was doing life right.

"I'd been bred for independence. The women in my extended family were all capable ladies, the energy, the force of their family units, the ones who got things done. My mother's highest hope for my younger siblings and me had always been that we would be able to stand on our own. You remember my baby journal I told you about?"

"The one your mother shared with you a few years ago?"

"Yeah. I wish I had it here to show you. The entries paint such a picture—it's the tale of a child being diligently primed for independence. Oh, wait! You know what?" I grabbed for my phone, "I think I emailed the pdf of the journal to myself at some point. Hold on, let me do a quick search...Yes! Oh my gosh, here it is! Okay, let me just read you a few:

> August 30, 1984—(4 ½ mos) This is so strange! Kristen has been exhibiting some signs of a new stage, but it seems to be very early for her to be in a "mommy cling." The last couple of days she has started crying when I left her alone. As soon as I picked her up she would stop. I thought (and read) this usually doesn't happen until 6 or 7 mo. But it seems, as usual, our bundle is ahead of the books. I don't feel good when she does this, though many books say mothers like this stage because they're the only ones who can calm the baby and feel needed, but I want her to be more independent and go to others easily. I know this is only a stage and I'll probably miss it when it's over.
>
> September 9, 1984—(5 mos) Today was Grandma's surprise party. There were about 60 people—mostly relatives. Kristen was in her play pen for a bout 10 min before a cousin went to pick her up and from that

moment on she wasn't put down. It was a LONG day and she was shuttled from person to person, but Kristen was wonderful. She did not cry even once!

September 16, 1984—(5 mos) A FIRST—I went to exercise class today and saw a lot of kids Kristen's age in walkers, so when we got home I dragged hers out. Boy, did she catch on fast! Kristen obviously liked her new freedom and independence and wanted to explore everything. I really felt a loss at seeing her wheel around exploring with no need of me, but I also felt a real thrill seeing her discover this new mobility and the fact that she could do it _herself_.

Dr. Sparrow took in the words with her usual open countenance, "Your mother does seem to be particularly focused on independence in those entries." Her eyebrows knit together in the effort of recall, "Haven't you also mentioned before that she didn't want your sister or you to be dependent on a husband?"

"The teaching certificate thing, yeah. Even after thirty years of marriage, and a full-time motherdom, she has never failed to remind us that she always kept her teaching certificate up to date, 'because you just never know when you're going to need to go out and support yourself.'" I shifted on the couch. "But, you know, I get it. My mom was wholly self-sufficient impossibly young. She was the only kid she knew with two working parents when she was growing up—this would have been the mid 60s. She was perched atop a step stool cooking for her little brother at an age most kids are still getting their hand slapped for going too close to the stove. She doesn't talk about it, to her it just seems normal, I think, but I don't think her parents were around a lot. I think not counting on anyone was her survival skill. And, it's not like my dad was a slouch when it came to self-sufficiency either. He was a Chicago city kid with older parents. Between a blind father and a mother who'd never learned to drive, he pretty much grew up on public transportation and pick up baseball games. The man had a paper route at ten. By the time he was twelve he'd fallen into the role of highly-responsible family coordinator."

"It makes sense that you value independence, then."

"Yeah. I've always liked the freedom that's come with being a 'capable girl.' I still do. But, at some point this vulnerability thing blipped on my radar. I think it was in high school that I began to get the impression that it was pretty essential because it was tied into the whole dating, relationship thing that was newly important to everyone. Listening to people talk, it seemed that if I wanted to have a boyfriend or husband someday—or even friend for that matter—this was a personality trait I was going to need. So, I put my mind to getting better at it.

"The way I was back then, that meant tackling vulnerability with the same resolute vigor I applied to my calculus homework." I grinned, the benefit of time and hindsight allowing me to enjoy the earnest if misguided thinking of my sixteen-year-old self. "As far as I could tell at the time, being vulnerable was the opposite of presenting my life as all sorted and shiny. So, I began a methodic campaign to share all of my off-putting character traits, my failures, anything that I wouldn't usually have advertised because it might have made me look bad. And as I remember it, I did this indiscriminately, telling anyone at school who'd listen—after all, if a little vulnerability was good for me, a ton was going to really humanize me to the world, right?"

Dr. Sparrow laughed. I felt pleased and continued, "Obviously, I didn't see any major change in my relationships—no boyfriend appeared to compliment me on my sexy vulnerability—but blindly assuming this was what was required of me, I stuck by a policy of brutal transparency for nearly a decade. It wasn't until I met with Dr. Patricia for the first time that I was confronted with an entirely new understanding of what it meant to be vulnerable."

I paused and took a sip from my water bottle. I pulled my legs up to sit cross legged on the couch. When I was again settled facing

Dr. Sparrow she prompted me to continue, "And what did you discover?"

I stared past Dr. Sparrow's head as I often did while collecting my thoughts in this room, letting my focus extend past the glass door behind her into the inviting scene of the backyard. Some days my attention was pulled there by the neighbor's cat walking by carrying a bird in its mouth. Once the sight of a massive raccoon lumbering past in broad daylight stopped me mid-sentence. Today, though, only hummingbirds flitted through the frame.

"I was twenty-seven by then. I started seeing Dr. Patricia after everything had fallen apart with Amanda." Dr. Sparrow nodded. "I thought time would just solve that heartbreak the way it was supposed to, but nine months had passed, and I was still spending ninety percent of my day thinking about her. She was my first thought in the morning, the last at night. Nothing seemed to be getting easier. I still felt like a walking wound, raw and open, like it had just happened. Like any minute I might figure out what I had done wrong and would be allowed to fix it. Like she might come back. Take me back. The pain was physical and would take my breath away with no warning ten times a day. I didn't know how to fix it. My brain. It was a looping tape recorder, and the buttons were jammed.

"Finally reaching out to Dr. Patricia, walking in to meet her that first session—sitting in that chair, facing another human being whom I immediately liked, and admitting that I was broken, that I wasn't strong enough to get over this one myself, that I needed help—specifically her help—that elicited a full terror response in my body. I was certain that once spoken aloud, this exposure of my need for her would leave me a shamed, quivering heap on the carpet. And I'd 'known,' in my twisty understanding of the way the world worked at the time, that in the face of my pathetic-ness, my desperate neediness, this kind, lovely stranger sitting across from me would leave, disgusted, and disappointed by my weakness.

"And I wouldn't have blamed her; I knew I was pathetic. But if she rejected me I felt it might actually kill me. Yes, I believed she would have been completely justified in walking out of the room in the face of my neediness, but I *wanted* her to stay. I *wanted* her to deem me worthy of her help. I *wanted* her not to give upon me, no matter how absurd and ridiculous that hope seemed at the time.

"In acknowledging that fragile, tender, fledgling *want*, I moved into deeper relationship with vulnerability." Dr. Sparrow waited silently for me to continue. I shook my head, emerging from my reverie. "After that experience, I was able to see that the adolescent 'sharing' I'd been doing of my less-than-shiny self for what it really had been: an act not of vulnerability but of strong-willed defiance. I'd been confronting people with my flaws, thrusting my mistakes at them and practically daring them to judge me, to leave me, with this thought of, *And, you know what? Good riddance if they do because it means they weren't real friends anyway. I'll be just fine without them.* I'd been risking nothing. Not really. My experience working with Dr. Patricia—it woke me up to the fact that true vulnerability requires *risk*. And risk is predicated by a genuinely desired outcome. I had to want her to stay in order to feel the risk that she might go. I had to admit I needed her help in order to experience genuine vulnerability."

Dr. Sparrow's clear-eyed nod spoke to the truth of my half-decade-old revelation. "Yes, we are vulnerable any time we express what we need from another." Her tone shifted from agreement to exploration, "Do you see, though, where there is a distinction between *neediness* and *having needs?* You're right that neediness can be problematic, but everyone has needs. A healthy relationship is one in which we are able to express our needs to one another and expect that they will be met. Or, at least, heard and considered."

"Sure. Yeah. Yeah, of course." I reflexively accepted her premise without feeling a connection to the truth in her statement. My mouth kept producing words as my mind scanned the mental cliff-face for the next handhold. "I mean, we've talked in here about the fact that what was so revolutionary about my experience with Naomi was the fact that I actually *did* feel allowed to have needs in our relationship.

I mean, I asked her to commit to our partnership! And even though she turned me down and I ultimately ended up here with you, I still had two years of experiencing someone meeting my needs, needs I'd been told were 'too much' my whole life. And it wasn't like I could only ask for things when there was a crisis. Practical stuff like admitting that I wanted her to take me to the airport or cook us breakfast. I was able to ask for time together, closeness. And what shocked me, what made me believe I could want partnership at all, was that over and over again she met those needs! She surpassed them, anticipated them time and again. Our relationship felt so safe that I was allowed to be vulnerable and risk showing up fully and admit to all of my wants. And miraculously, I never felt needy—"

My mouth snapped shut in a full stop, and my eyes focused on some unseen object in the space between us. Something was coming together.

My entire life I'd felt I been doing relationship wrong. I either wasn't dating enough or correctly or was too affectionate with my friends or didn't show interest in the opposite sex. I had become too loyal to some while overlooking others' very existence. Despite that, I had managed to experience some amazing, dear, nourishing relationships through the course of my life. In fact, I could point immediately to the most influential and important relationships that had come across my path over time, and in this instant, I could see that they all had a bizarre commonality: each had suffered the tinge of 'wrongness.'

The relationships that I most valued, those in which I had felt the most loved and seen, these had been the relationships I'd felt compelled to protect, to hide from the prying, judgmental eyes of others. Some part of me had been certain that if anyone found out how close, how emotionally intimate, how much I needed these relationships, I would have been scolded and made to look on, my head hung in helpless shame, as they were taken away from me like a toy from a naughty child.

Like most life-changing insights, the one that was coming

together as I sat there on Dr. Sparrow's couch would eventually seem almost ridiculously obvious. Even in the moment I wondered how I hadn't seen it before. I'd had all the individual puzzle pieces to understand the big picture for years. Yet, the entire cast of seemingly independent players had chosen 1:45 PM on this unremarkable Monday for a curtain call, emerging onto the stage all at once, allowing me to see the integral roles they'd played in the theatre of my life.

There was no warning of the sob that violently burst through me, but it took me for only a moment before I found myself again stoic. Stunned. I tried to look at Sparrow, but it was like trying to force the North ends of two magnets together. I couldn't pull my sightline up to meet hers. I could feel thickening words still a jumbled mess in my mouth, and they would not be pushed out prematurely. Reactively my hands flew up, gripping either side of my forehead like a vice in response to a sudden pain there. I swore I could *feel* my brain rewiring, the synaptic patterns jumping out of their well-worn ruts, new bridges and connections coming on line. More tears stung my eyes, silently this time. Then, again, stillness. My hands drifted back down to my lap. A shuttering breath was followed by my slow, clear voice.

"What if somewhere along the line my wiring got crossed, and my brain labeled needing others—in any capacity—as 'wrong,' as shameful? What if every intimate relationship that felt 'wrong,' that felt like I needed to protect it and keep it secret, felt that way because I was *actually showing up* in it, wholly vulnerable and free to acknowledge that I had needs?"

The past is defined by the present. My past cascaded like a deck of cards into a new shuffle, a new configuration of Truth. "That would mean the relationships that have felt most forbidden to me have really been the healthiest relationships I've ever had." My eyes finally locked back onto Dr. Sparrow's. "That changes everything."

Data Analysis:

Love demands vulnerability. I was blind to what it looked like to be vulnerable, but I *could* identify those seemingly mystical relationships in which I felt truly nourished. We all know which human connections light us up and make us feel worthy. What I had never understood was *why* those particular relationships had made me feel like the best version of myself. It turned out that they provided me the opportunity to be vulnerable, to show up wholly myself.

We cannot force vulnerability, we can't fake it, we can only allow for its appearance. During a lifetime of actively attempting to 'make' myself vulnerable, genuine vulnerability had snuck in the side door alongside Love. The first indication that I was misunderstanding vulnerability as a young person should have been the mere fact that I indiscriminately shared my failures with anyone who would listen. Being vulnerable by communicating our wants is risky, compounded by a second layer of implied desire—for that nascent aspect of self, that unspoken want, to be respectfully and tenderly accepted by the receiver.

When in a state of genuine vulnerability, we identify intuitively those who are simply not appropriate midwifes for our fledgling desires. We recognize them in those moments of leaving lunch with a friend and noting that we never brought up the new boyfriend, or wondering how we managed to spend an entire afternoon with family without mentioning the dance lessons we're taking, stand-up comedy we're doing, book we're writing.

Inversely, when I witness myself interacting again and again with someone in a state of easy vulnerability, I know I've found something truly special. In an unexpected turnabout, now that I am able to recognize it, my experience of vulnerability within a relationship— the frequency with which I share my needs, the freedom I feel around showing up 'as is,' and yes, even the arrival of that outdated, misfiring feeling of 'wrongness'—has become my canary in the coal mine. Its presence alerts me to a very important fact, a fact I spent most of my life missing. It lets me know I've found healthy resonance with another.

I had been working from a place of either or—I could either be vulnerable and thereby in partnership or I could be strong and independent and make my mark in the world as a useful member of society. But now I could see that was a constructed binary. Healthy partnership had made me feel *more* myself, *more* capable and supported in my endeavors. Vulnerability didn't make me weak, it made me stronger. I could have both. I wanted both.

Conclusion:

There is a term in Sanskrit *neti, neti* which literally translates to "not that, not that" and essentially means "sometimes it's easier to explain something by what it's not than by what it is." Vulnerability is not the act of revealing all of the worst aspects of ourselves to those we hold dear, though occasionally sharing things we'd rather keep hidden from view can be part of the process. It is not synonymous with high emotion or soap-opera level dramatics, though it can choose to wear those adornments at times. Vulnerability is not neediness, though it is often present in the moments we admit to feeling needy. Vulnerability is not weakness, for nothing that takes such bravery could be.

My teacher Ravi Ravindra once gave a talk called *Science and the Sacred*. In it he shared that the definition of "experiment" is to control conditions and put another in peril, whereas "experience" is defined as putting oneself in peril. Many of us spend most of our adult lives running experiments in vulnerability. To experience it requires a genuine risking of self. This means showing up as ourselves in relationship. It means making the choice to not self-protect when an uncomfortable moment arises in which we are asked to pull back the curtain to reveal a part of our inner workings. It's admitting to ourselves that we desire something. It's admitting to another that we have a need, dream, want, and that they have a role to play.

Vulnerability cannot show up in the vacuum of apathy. Its appearance requires us to first claim our stake in the ground. It's, "I want that role so I can hear the applause," rather than "Sure, it'd be cool but, you know, I just auditioned for fun." "I want to get that promotion and have my value recognized," as opposed to, "It's no big deal whether I get it; it's not like I need more work anyway." It's, "Please, stay. I want you to stay," not, "No, yeah, that's fine. Go. Stay. Whatever you want is cool." It's foregoing, "Yeah, hey, listen, if love shows up one day, great. And if it doesn't I'm totally fine on my own," if we don't mean it and instead claiming, "I want a partner, a teammate, I want to know that kind of love. I want it with you."

Sometimes we don't feel a strong want. That's normal. Those simply aren't the scenarios in which vulnerability can present herself; she can't get a foothold. Vulnerability is predicated by want—usually a want we've kept under wraps from others or, often, ourselves—because in order for us to *risk* something we have to first *want* something, and true vulnerability requires risk. Risking the acknowledgement of our want to ourselves or to another is the crux of stepping into genuine vulnerability.

Love demands vulnerability. Vulnerability requires risk. Risk necessitates want. So, let's start there.

Run Your Own Experiment No. 14:

The purpose of this experiment is to identify our accessible vulnerabilities so that we can begin to practice safe sharing and connection within relationship.

Experimental Procedure:

1. Return to the list of wants you wrote in experiment No. 10.

2. Take this opportunity to write each item in the form of, "I want a relationship/ marriage/partnership that _____." Add any new wants that you have identified.

3. Now, rewrite this list of sentences with the new prefix, "[Your Name] will never have a relationship/marriage/partnership that _____."

4. Read this second list aloud.

5. If certain sentences move you, elicit fear or shame, make you feel beaten or sad or rile you to defiance, acknowledge that fact without judgement. Simply record the data that these are aspects that you strongly desire to have present in your life.

6. Choose one item from the list that elicited a strong response and share it with someone you trust to help you hold intention for this fledgling desire.

7. Do your best to stay present with all of the physical sensations and emotions that arise as you share. Let this be a mindful practice of becoming familiar with what genuine vulnerability feels like for you.

CHAPTER FIFTEEN

Enjoy a State of Eternal Self-Hypothesis

hy·poth·e·sis /hīˈpäTHəsəs/:
a supposition or proposed explanation made on the basis of limited evidence as a starting point for further investigation; an assumption or concession made as a basis for reasoning, for the sake of argument.

SUBJECT: Overthinker; Female; Age 34 years, 17 days.

HYPOTHESIS: I experiment in order to understand my world as a series of concrete, stable, and unchanging truths.

METHOD: Competitive transformation, Earth's orbit, *The Lego Movie.*

FIELD SITE: A nice, though non-descript, airport hotel conference room.

Experiment 180.42.4:

"So, we're going to go around the room and name one area of our lives in which we want to experience authentic success."

The, "Aw, geeze," flew out of my mouth like a reflex. We'd been asked to plumb much deeper depths than this over the course of the weekend retreat, so I couldn't explain the wave of nerves that instantly put my body on edge.

"Now, you're not choosing the *only* area," the couple leading this exercise stood at the head of our U-shaped tables. They attempted to out-speak the nervous titter that now filled the room, "Hopefully you get to have authentic success in all areas of your lives, but choose the *one* right now that feels juicy for you because we're going to work with it in our next exercise."

Okay, this should be simple enough. I know the answer to this one already, right? Over the past few months two themes had been in the forefront of my mind, the desire for partnership and the desire for tribe. I said each word internally, feeling into which rang truest in my body. *'I want partnership.' 'I want tribe.'*

Yeah, it's definitely partnership.

"Jennifer, let's start with you and go around."

The woman at the top of the U took a breath that telegraphed the deep truth of whatever was about to come out of her mouth. "I want to experience authentic success in a loving partnership."

Oh! She took ours.

I laughed at myself internally. *As though originality counts in our deepest desires. As though we aren't all looking for the same exact things.* The room was full of coaches, healers, and counselors I'd come to know through this class over the previous year. I'd had heartfelt connections with most, so the revealing thought that I might 'copy' another's deep truth felt doubly amusing. Jennifer handed the mic to Pastor Hazel, and I continued my internal conversation.

Let's just double check that it's really 'partnership.'

By all means. We should feel certain. Go ahead. There's still lots of time.

"I want to feel authentic success that I've provided for my children after I die."

I was seated at the turn of the U, a little past the half way point of this gathering of three dozen or so. I remained present with others' answers while I poked and prodded the dense fog of feeling churning in my belly, searching for just the right word that both lit me up and scared me a little.

"I want to feel I'm living my purpose."

You're right, it does seem to be in the 'partnership' lane, but that's not quite complete either, is it? It's something more.

As was the trend with this group, answers became more lengthy as the mic made its slow progression. Occasionally the couple up front would challenge an answer, dragging it out of the theoretically ethereal to ground it in reality.

"I'd like to experience authentic success in my abundance."

"Abundance of what?"

"Abundance of resources."

"What resources?"

"Financial resources."

"So you'd like to have money. Cash."

"Ack! Yes." Laughter.

"Okay, *claim* that then!"

Let's remember what it felt like to be in partnership with Naomi, and maybe we can identify what we want to replicate.

My body dropped into the feeling-memory on command. I was thankful that enough time had passed that I had access to the good times again.

There's joy. Relief.

Why relief?

Because there was security.

My chest felt full with the expansive freedom of deep mutual commitment.

'Marriage!' That's the word!

My friend Cam two seats over took the mic.

That's the word! Wow. Yes, you're right, that feels true. 'I want authentic success in marriage.'

Whoa. Are we really going to say that out loud?

The confession definitely ticked the boxes of both exciting and frightening. I returned my attention to Cam who was standing now making her claim. "I intend to find authentic success in relationship." There was a half-beat of silence in which we all observed our teachers' unconvinced looks. Our eyes returned to Cam expectantly. She broke into an embarrassed grin and blurted, "Well, I mean, I want *marriage*, but I've never actually *said* that before!" The room broke out in laughter and applause.

No way.

"Okay, so let's pause here a moment because I think you need to really claim this…" As Cam was guided towards the truth of her confession, my insides prodded anew. *Is that really my word? Did she read my mind? Or did I read hers?*

I repeated and tested the word that had popped simultaneously into my head and out of Cam's mouth. In search of the truest truth, my body again time-traveled to the best of times with Naomi. I luxuriated in the sensations of having a primary partner, my person, of being someone's person. I felt the strong one–on–one connection with another, joyful in the tie that bound us together.

Then my perspective broadened of its own volition. In my mind's eye I looked down and saw my son. I felt the strength of my connection with him. Next, I looked over at the tether I shared with a dear high school friend. And then my closest mom-friend. And another, and another, exponentially. I felt all the chords of intimacy emanating from me into the landscape of people in my life. I was in the experience of all of my relationships, each one safely in their silo. Protected from and unaffected by one another. Each contained within their individual lane in neat and orderly fashion.

I was only vaguely aware when Cam took her seat and handed the mic to the woman seated between us. I was occupied, experiencing the configurations of my relationships growing, pushing through their constraints, overflowing their boundaries to co-mingle, to become a huge mesh of interconnectedness. A mad, messy, wonderful web of relationships.

And just like that, I had my word. It was inarguable. So much so that I began to shiver. The shiver became a full shake. I wrapped my arms around myself tightly in a vain attempt to minimize my conspicuousness. *Okay, this reaction is good. This is just my physiology confirming that we're in new territory.* I dropped my gaze when the tears started leaking out, trying not to distract from the woman next to me who was now sharing. *My body is simply working out a deep physiological release of old beliefs. Let it happen. These people will understand.* The therapist sitting to my right, a sweet woman in her fifties, observed what was happening and placed a steadying hand on my back, but my shoulders only shook harder with each passing moment. I was quickly losing it. *Should I run out of the room? Give up and collapse? She's going to hand me the mic any second. I have no idea what I'm going to do.*

That's okay. We don't have to know.

When my turn came I didn't pretend I wasn't in the throes of something. I couldn't. This was the boon of being in a room full of people who made it their life's work to be open, curious, accepting. I knew I was safe. I didn't have to waste energy on managing myself which was good because it took every bit of what I had left to get this one word out. I brought the microphone to my chin and spoke it into the room. "Family."

Data Analysis:

A chiropractor once explained to me that whiplash injuries are not a result of a sudden change in the position of the head in an accident. It turns out the human spine is actually designed to handle a quick force change, the vertebra rolling languidly to compensate, the neck allowing the head to move from back to forward and back again, held and cushioned by a flexible and supportive spine. Injury occurs when this natural pivot of direction, this smooth and ready response, is *interrupted*. It's when the second car collides with the first, and the flow of the spine in its graceful dance of bounce and recoil is jarred, not allowed to complete its flawless nimble redirection. We are naturally designed to handle quick shifts, surprising changes, unforeseen course corrections with grace and ease. Problems arise only when there is forceful resistance, when our innate ability to gracefully incorporate change is interrupted, when we go rigid.

I used to suffer every time something wasn't going to plan. My control was challenged by every deviation, my safety threatened. The awe-inspiring surprises of this life, the un-knowable, un-plan-able, totally chaotic-seeming moments, felt like a disruption. Now, here I sat able to see the neat order I'd imposed upon my relationships, neatly keeping each separate and controlled, and I found myself craving the breakdown of these walls. I ached for the interconnected weave of true family.

And perhaps this is what my relationship with Naomi and the experience of being a mother have clarified most for me. The feeling of family.

Family, in my estimation, is based in a shared priority: the health of the Family. I imagine it kind of like an amoeba with a bunch of arms. Keeping that amoeba healthy and thriving means every part of it gets to be healthy and thriving. Family is the collaborative project that is being crafted, built, cared for, and tended by those involved. We have agreed that this Family is the most important thing for all of our individual health, and we are committed to its nurturing.

My family in the truest sense of the word today consists of myself and my son, and it is a beautiful experience for me. It's a particularly potent illustration because I have unequivocally committed myself to our family's growth and health, but in his four-year-old mind, our family is not merely the most important thing in the world, it IS the world. I've found that the innate level of all-in-ness coming from his little being ratchets my game way up to meet him in his devotion to our shared project of Family.

Being able to identify my experience of Family in this way also clarifies some of my own values and behavior, namely honesty, transparency, and compiling of resources. I think my compulsive and immediate offering of my resources—be they skills, financial, homes, offices, my physical self or contacts I've cultivated—has been an unconscious desire to build family. I've been wanting to be in the all-in joyful, useful, committing of resources with others who are equally all-in.

Likewise, to skillfully nurture Family with my other team members, I feel the need for everyone to be all in when it comes to information. All of the members of a family, each flange if you will, is out in the world gathering information. It benefits the family to bring all of that information back to the amoeba so that we can together be clearer, better informed, better equipped to navigate the world. This includes the state of each person's physical and mental health. If information is being hidden out of fear or embarrassment, then the team members are making decisions with only partial data. It's like a patient asking a doctor to heal them while at the same time not disclosing a critical piece of their medical history. If, however, the team members are committed to consistently sharing data and pooling knowledge and resources, then more informed choices and better decisions can be made, and the health of the Family will be served. I want my family to feel they can be transparent with their feelings, their experiences, their hurts and their joys. I want us to be communicating when internal shifts are happening, when life circumstances are changing, when illness hits, when jobs are lost, when that habit that used to be adorable has become annoying, when a mistake has been made, when an opportunity has arisen. That is the pact I want for my family.

My ability to desire family over control that day in the conference room was a huge indicator that something fundamental had shifted within me. It told me that I was no longer under the impression that I had to use my overthinker's skills to control the world around me with white knuckled precision in order to keep myself safe.

For years I drove around with a sturdy little green duffel

wedged behind the bench seat of my two-seater truck. I dubbed this permanent fixture my Just-In-Case bag. At any given moment, you could find it stocked with:

» 1 pair of high heels
» 1 pair of cheap flip flops
» 1 work dress (wrinkle free)
» 1 tank top
» 1 bra
» 1 pair of shorts
» 1 pair of comfy underwear
» 1 thong
» 1 swim suit
» 1 beach towel
» 1 hair brush
» 4 hair ties
» 3 tampons
» 5 twenty dollar bills
» 5 one gallon ziplock bags (for wet suits or sandy flip flops)
» 1 overnight kit (tooth brush, toothpaste, tweezers, Q-tips)

This little bag of overthinker planning gave me the freedom to immediately say 'yes!' to an impromptu trip to the beach or an invitation to after-work drinks without so much as a second thought. It is a perfect example of my overthinker's superpowers working in service not of the illusion of control, but of the truth that I don't know what adventure lies around the corner. Nowadays, I don't even want to know. The surprise has always been so much better than what I could have imagined for myself.

I love being an overthinker. I love plans and preparation, systems and patterns and order because they are no longer rigid hindrances but tools that allow me to more easily say 'yes' to my life. It's the means by which I can jump into the unknown, the unexpected, uncertain, messy, enriching adventures of life. The greatest and messiest of which is this: Family.

Conclusion:

There was a time when our species knew that the Earth was flat. It was just fact. Then we discovered it was round, and we were at the center of the universe. Just look, you can see the Sun moving around us in the sky. Duh.

Well, we know how that turned out.

As overthinkers, there is a temptation not to act until we feel certain all of the data is in. The thing is, until we kick the bucket and launch off this earthly realm, there will be a never-ending onslaught of new data coming in. We cannot know ourselves the way we know that 2 + 2 is 4. Self-knowledge is not a task to accomplish. There is no moment in which we are able to say, "Okay, finally, I know myself now. Check. Done. What's next?" We are constantly interpolating new data, running new experiments, encountering new variables; and this changes us, who we are, how we feel, what we think daily, minute to minute.

So, what are we going to do, stand frozen in the illusion that we've somehow paused life? How, if we stop, are we supposed to generate the new data we're supposedly awaiting? In these moments, the world is still turning, the forces of the Universe are still in full motion, but we've simply chosen to stop engaging in the experiment. We've decided to put on our blinders and freeze in favor of the thought that we might be in control of our one little miniscule corner of existence.

That's what our overthinking really comes down to, doesn't it? Control. It's the thought that we can keep ourselves safe and protected from the chaos that lurks outside of our front door. On some level it's such an appealing daydream, the image of our rational and methodically laid plans buoying us through this life right over the mess and confusion of humanity. The problem is that in this daydream we remain separate from the world rather than engaged participants. And if what we desire is love and relationship, maintaining this separateness is an anathema to fulfilling our dreams.

Joseph Campbell is credited with saying, "We must be willing to get rid of the life we've planned, so as to have the life that is waiting for us." It doesn't sound so different from Jesus' assertion that we must forsake our former life when the calling of a new one comes knocking, or the yogis' meditations on non-attachment. The wisdom seems universal: Don't get so blindly bound up by your plans that you miss your life. If Alexander Flemming returned from holiday and simply chucked the blue-green mold covered petri dish he found awaiting him as an unacceptable deviation from his designed experiment, we might still be regularly dying from run of the mill bacterial infections for lack of penicillin.

When the goal is control, every unknown threatens that. Everything that has, is, and will ever occur throughout the course of our lives, becomes an attack on our plans. Life becomes an attack, and we become the victim. Victims of the world that keeps messing with our concretized plans. Eternally.

When in this victim mentality, no matter what our age, we can't act as adults with agency in our lives. When we are in the mode of thinking like a victim—protective, defensive, focused only on identifying the perpetrator who wronged us and seeking the external cause of our pain—we are incapable of giving and receiving love.

A wise man once told me that the only way out of victimhood is acceptance. Not of what we wish it was or think it should be, but of what is. That doesn't mean we have to agree with it, but we decide the consequence of our disagreement. Pain is objection to what is. Suffering is the choice we make to prolong that objection. We have all experienced unexpected course corrections of life and circumstance. A lost job, an illness, a promotion, a move, discovering that you've won the lottery, that your daughter is pregnant, that your wife is leaving, that your boyfriend wants to marry you, that you're in love, that you're not—these moments challenge our self-perception, our understanding of the way the world works, but it's our *response* to them that determines whether we end up suffering whiplash. Acceptance of what is (and our role in and responsibility for it) is what allows for accurate preparation and active engagement in our lives. It's what allows our skills as overthinkers to be in service of the correct master. Not control. Preparation for the next grand unknown adventure awaiting us just around the corner.

Getting ourselves ready for relationship is preparing for the greatest unknown. Until we are able to join the present moment, accept what is whether we agree with it or not, and choose our next action as a responsible adult, we are unable to participate in a healthy relationship. Misapplying our overthinking as a way to control our own safety makes us rigid, and rigidity is relationship kryptonite. It cuts us off from the flexibility required for human relationship. Anyone who thinks they're going to enter partnership, define all the parameters and behaviors, dynamics and roles, record them in an owner's manual and put them on the shelf for reference is headed for a brutal awakening. But at the other extreme, taking an attitude of complete and total abdication of responsibility, expounding beliefs that, "Oh, whoever enters and exits my life is how it is meant to be, I have no say in the matter, so I'll just do me," cuts us off from the emotional investment and commitment structure required for meaningful partnership.

A relationship is a living, growing organism. It needs both space to grow organically and skillful responsive support to thrive. If you've seen *The Lego Movie*, you already know what I'm talking about. There were two camps of thought in Lego City, those who valued creativity above all else, and those who valued rule-following as king. In the face of crisis, the hyper-creative master builders were unable to work together, and the by-the-book instruction followers were unable to innovate. It took both aspects coming together to save their world and build a functional society (and, incidentally, allow for a loving relationship between father and son to flourish).

This is where the tools and tendencies toward organization, preparedness, overthinking fulfill their true purpose, when they act as the skills that allow us to meet life's unanticipated moments, new relationships, potential intimacies, momentary expressions of love, unexpected connections and kindnesses with delight and joy and a big fat, 'Yes!' Planning is not a skill to hone as a way to pre-ordain our lives in the theoretical, but to allow us to meet them fully in reality.

Know Thyself is, more accurately, a command to a state of being: an open-ended state of self-hypothesis. To be eternally self-curious is to be eternally delighted by unexpected data, by our reactions and thoughts, by what we discover anew within our thoughts and desires. "I don't know what's next," is not a state of waiting. It's the reality of living everyday. So let's take stock of our data, and begin building the framework now for the love and the life that awaits us just around the bend.

Run Your Own Experiment No. 15:

The purpose of this experiment is to identify places in our lives where our rigid planning is fighting our ability to identify opportunities for relationship.

Experimental Procedure:

1. Bring to mind a place in your life where you have felt like the victim of outside forces, be it an individual, group, society in general, or even yourself.

2. In one to two paragraphs, write out a paired down narrative of what was done to you and how it blocked you from the things you were trying to accomplish.

3. Now, step back from the narrative you've written so that you are no longer the lead character, but the omniscient and benevolent author who wants nothing but the best for the subject of the story.

4. Write one to two paragraphs, either imagined or based in real-world outcomes, about how this apparent block or disruption actually helped your lead character. Perhaps it set them on a new path, opened unexpected opportunities, or led them to make a new friend.

5. Can you see how your lead character may have missed the signs that what was happening was in their own interest? Take this mentality into the world today. When something occurs that feels like a block to your plans, pause and imagine a story where the outcome of this apparent derailment might lead you into a moment of serendipity.

CHAPTER SIXTEEN
Let Love Be a Life Catalyst

cat·a·lyst /ˈkad(ə)ləst/:
a substance that enables a chemical reaction
to proceed at an unusually faster rate or under
different conditions than otherwise possible; an
agent that provokes significant change or action

SUBJECT: Overthinker; Female; Age 34 years, 5 months.

HYPOTHESIS: I recognize where I feel incomplete, so I seek to
call in a partner who will complete those aspects of myself.

METHOD: A career change, 1990s television, two water glasses.

FIELD SITE: A small metal tube hurtling over the globe at 500
miles per hour.

Experiment 180.90.1:

"So, there I am sitting on the plane, wondering what was next with
my career. Kicking around the fact that I seem to restart something

new every couple years. Feeling like again I'm back at square one. And I said to myself in just this musing way, *What if I just accepted the fact that I'm not good at making money?* It would be so amazing to just drop the charade that I ever was going to be getting some big paycheck. And then I thought how amazing it would be to just follow whatever work was interesting without regard to what it paid.

"Imagining such a thing was felt so freeing, but you know, impossible. It'd be one thing if it were just me, but I have a kid. Then I thought, *Well, if I was in a partnership where my partner had an amazing job that could actually be the case. It's not so ludicrous a notion. Tons of people are in marriages where one person is bringing home the paycheck. Who's to say I'd have to be the one earning all the money in our family?*

"I was totally horrified! What this voice was suggesting was that I have the kind of marriage arrangement I'd left back in the Midwest—casting me as some kind of homemaker and my spouse as breadwinner—I recoiled at the thought of being a part of this image I'd come to think of as old fashioned and disempowering. I had such an intense automatic reaction, in fact, that I caught it as it was happening. I was fascinated and decided to move towards it. I started to play with this 'normal' family image. I couldn't argue that my assumption that I was going to spend my life in an eternal struggle to find soul-nourishing work that also paid suddenly seemed like only one of many different realistic permutations.

"And here's the thing I need to fill you in on. What I've recognized recently from my work history is that my default when I connect with someone is All In. It's like, 'Hi! We are now in relationship. Here are all of my resources and gifts for you to access. Mi casa es su casa, and my greatest joy is in finding ways to make your life easier and your day better!' I'm not saying that in a martyr-y way. It's just what I can see I've done over and over and over again in my life—reflexively, automatically. It's my nature. And in every one of these cases where an opportunity arose to work with the person I was connected to, it was like, 'Oh, wonderful! A codified way for me to *really* make your life easier and for all of my resources to be put towards something creative we can build and birth together. Of course, yes!'

"And each time I've done that it's been *amazing* for a year or two, but then something gets out of whack. Things begin to feel uneven. I begin to feel taken advantage of because now, here I am in a working relationship that should be based on an equal exchange of skills for money, and instead it's totally out of balance. By the time I feel this way though, there's no fixing it. In making their life as easy as possible, in working around them, I've bred a situation where I've never asked anything of them, and now they can't deliver whatever I need for me to do my job well. It becomes glaringly obvious all of a sudden that I've been all in with someone who's been revealed as just a co-worker. And they're not all in— appropriately so—I'm the one out of step, but we're totally out of balance. I've set myself up to be the less loved, less desired, less cared for partner over and over.

"So, this is part of why I've been nervous about taking on whatever's next with work—this awareness that I need to be vigilantly self-policing so I don't fall into that pattern again. Here's why I'm telling you all of this: When I allowed myself to actively envision being with a partner who was providing for our family financially, immediately I felt totally free to be as All In as I could ever want to be. I felt no fear. No imbalance. I realized that my All In-ness was not actually a liability, but that it could be beautiful when in the correct container of romantic partnership. In thirty-four years I've never been in a romantic partnership. I've been trying to squish all that energy into improper containers.

"What's even more amazing, is that because I now had this highly successful provider avatar partner available to my imagination, the next scene it spontaneously conjured up was me sitting on the beach on family vacation watching my father talk business with her. They had this matter-of-fact mutual respect thing happening that made me feel so at ease. It took me totally by surprise because no matter how I've tried, I've NEVER been able to imagine my parents interacting in any way with a partner."

"So, it is a woman you're envisioning?" Dr. Sparrow asked without prejudice.

"That's what came through that day. I can't say for *certain* that I'm not simply sensing the feminine aspect of a man, of course, but I saw my wife."

"So, tell me about her."

"She's in her late thirties, a few years older than I am, or maybe just feels mature. She's been successful in her career. She's wanting a family. She's intelligent and kind. Responsible. Athletic. She is pleased to be able to provide for us. She's confident and capable. She's happy to have me be her cheerleader. She's appreciates all of my energy and joy in providing a beautiful home for us, in making her life, our lives more lovely. She loves my son. Loves our family. She trusts God's plan. She values commitment. She communicates and strives for clarity. She's a seeker." I stopped there, awaiting a reaction.

"Earlier I asked you what you wanted more of in your life, your vision for who you were moving into being. You used nearly every adjective you just listed. Do you realize that you've just described yourself? Your not-so-future self, maybe. Though I bet if you asked the you that existed a few years ago to look at who you are as you sit here now, you'd fit the bill entirely." I blinked in silent response. "Kristen, what if you are the very person you've been searching for?"

Data Analysis:

I've witnessed two demonstrations of partnership involving water glasses, and when I put them together I find them to be particularly illustrative. Most of us are partially filled glasses of water. We all want to be full. When two partially filled glasses meet, each wants the other to fill them up. So, the first pours some of its water into the second. But now the first is even more depleted, so the second pours some water into the first. But now the second is in greater need. And back and forth it goes with neither getting full, both feeling they need the other to become full, and the water in each slowly turning bitter with resentment.

Now see in front of you two glasses filled to the brim with water, so much so that they actually overflow and the saucers they sit upon are also filled up. These glasses meet. Neither needs anything from the other, and each can give and take the overflow of one another's saucers without depleting the other's fullness. This is healthy partnership. This is what I want for myself.

In my formative years I fed on a steady diet of 1990s television. Favorite shows like *The Nanny* and *Who's the Boss?*, *X-Files* and *The West Wing*, that revolved around years-long will-they-won't-they dynamics between two characters who, for various reasons, couldn't be together. I was completely riveted by these extended courtships, gazing with near-worship up at the screen, replaying each 'almost' moment in my head over and over. I dreamed of experiencing something like it in my own life, but I categorized these thoughts as frivolous fantasies. Because their dependence upon some outside person magically appearing by chance to deliver this desired courtship. It left my fate in the lap of another, and that felt suspiciously disempowering.

In my early thirties I read Robert A. Johnson's books, *She*, *We*, and *He*. I felt as though for the first time I understood what felt so off to me about this falling in love business. In *We* I learned that the whole idea of 'romantic love' was new and uniquely Western, born from the created concept of courtly love in the eleventh century through which knights chastely deified beautiful, married ladies of the court and fought for their honor. Over time this devotion to and deification of another grew to replace the role of religion in Western culture (while at the same time trading its chaste beginnings for sexual stirrings). Our devotion, and desire for purpose, ecstasy, and fullness, which had previously found satisfaction in the cathedral, now sought fulfillment in the idealization of an individual human being we were meant to 'have'. That's one heck of a case of mass transference.

In the final paragraphs of the book, Johnson points toward Eastern cultures, particularly those in which arranged marriage is still the norm, as a control variable. "They take the personified archetypes as symbols of another world and take each other as human beings...A man's commitment to his wife does not depend on his staying 'in love' with her. His relationship to his wife is based on loving *her*, not on being 'in love' with an ideal that he projects onto her." (p. 199) Johnson asserts that there is no confusion between the capabilities of a specific flawed human being with whom one chooses to build a loving, thriving family and the hunger for something to magically make us feel whole. Personal and spiritual fulfillment is appropriately addressed at the local temple, not the marriage bed.

Whether we're speaking of a temple, cathedral, or your version of spiritual seeking on the mountaintop is unimportant. What I understood in this passage was that this thing that had made no sense to me, the apparent truth I was being fed that falling in love would make me full—that I would be eternally incomplete if I did not partner—was finally spelled out as a Western myth. And, in fact, any thought that a partner could complete me—that another flawed human could step in and play the role of spiritual, psychological, and emotional healer—was a completely unfair and impossible standard to which to hold another human!

I no longer feel that wanting marriage casts me in the role of disempowered, helpless girl nor is it an embarrassing indicator that there are innate failures within me that need external solving. And likewise, relationship is no longer two people coming together to act as the missing puzzle pieces for one another, but as the strange and wonderful alchemy of two complete elements mixing to create a wholly new element.

Like the water glasses, I want to be a whole person, so full that I have a reservoir of overflowing love that I want to share with another, that I'm compelled to share it. It was this sentiment I heard ringing in the closing lines of *We*. "We can learn that the essence of love is not to use the other to make us happy but to serve and affirm the one we love. And we can discover, to our surprise, that what we have needed more than anything was not so much to be loved, as to love." (p. 201)

Conclusion:

It seems that most of us respond to our wish for a partner in one of two tracks. The first is what I'll call the Proactive Pursuer. Driven by a sense of taking matters into their own hands, these people run towards the dating scene looking for a person to quell their sense of lack. Usually directed by no intention more complex than 'to be partnered,' the Proactive Pursuer may partner often and badly because they are cut off from the specific needs they're looking to satisfy through partnership.

The second track is the Fatalist. These individuals often have a sense that their life would improve if they could find a partner, but the odds of that seem so slim as to make the entire partnering endeavor feel like a hopeless lottery. They feel powerless in the face of such odds and cut off from any agency to create a happy partnership. Very often, this type will simply refuse the idea of partnership the way most refuse the existence of fairies or UFOs.

The want of a partner need not manifest as a manic serial dating born of desperation for someone out there to fill all the missing parts of ourselves with their perfectly correlating puzzle pieces, nor as an outdated tableau of dramatic cries to the Universe, "Oh, why can't I find a (wo)man!?" There is one mistaken attitude that both the Proactive Pursuer and the Fatalist share. That is, each is under the impression that their life's happiness is contingent upon a partner's delivery of it.

It's no wonder so many of us feel embarrassment, or in my case outright shame, in confessing that we want to meet our partner when in either case we're admitting to the fact that we are lacking, and someone outside of us is the only one able to solve that lack. But with a slight reframe, we can experience this desire for a partner as the useful tool it is to gain self-awareness and agency in our lives. If we're able to recognize these waves of desire as good and valuable data, we can invite them in, converse with them, find out what needs are asking to be fulfilled beneath the surface external desire for a boyfriend or girlfriend, husband or wife. We can begin to see the desire for relationship as what it really is: a healthy, self-aware acknowledgement that there's something we want more of in our daily existence.

Think of it as if you were suddenly ravenous for a piece of cake. Rather than driving out to the store and plunging face first into some prepared confection you are able to step back and ask, "Why do I suddenly want cake so badly?" You may realize you forgot to eat breakfast this morning, and your body is in dire need of fuel. After a salad, a little protein, your system is happy. In this example, there is no need to mete out moral judge upon yourself for the fact that you experienced overwhelming desire for cake at 10:00 in the morning. *A stronger, more attractive, more evolved person wouldn't want cake. My desire for cake only evidences what a mess my life is!* Cake wasn't the need, it was just the loudest most straightforward flashcard your system could find to bat-signal into your brain and alert you to its need. Knowing that, you get to instead thank your psyche in the moment for so efficiently getting you the memo.

And, I feel it is important to note here that yes, sometimes we just want cake.

In the same way, we can look at strong desires for partnership as welcome messages from the deep that have surfaced to help us attune our life's compass. Peeking beneath the initial desire to discover the driving wishes we hold for ourselves can inform the jobs we take, the friendships we maintain, the situations in which we put ourselves, and the efforts we put forth lives. Wanting a partner or wanting something more in an existing partnership brings us again back to the importance of knowing what we want and letting that be the driving force for us to build the full life we desire for ourselves *this very moment.*

Knowing what you want from a partner is the doorway into acknowledging your own opportunities to build, a key to the code for your ultimate happiness. Maybe you'll meet Prince(ss) Charming, maybe you'll meet someone who meets most or some of the rainbow-unicorns vision of a partner. But even if you (or I) do, let's cut through the thought that another can be the ultimate answer to happiness or satisfaction. Because they're not a unicorn. They are human. They will fail. How much more gracious you can be with their failing if you're still feeling satisfied by the life you've built, the communities, situations, friends and family who help provide what you crave and enrich your life—if your cup is still full? The sound structure we build now allows us to hold for the creative chaos of love. How much longer that relationship will last. How much more love and less resentment.

Stop waiting around. You have agency now. Instead of desire making us blind, desperate, needy, pairing with the wrong person, let's allow it to bring clarity, information, clear seeing so that we may pair well and with far more flexibility and fun. You'll have more space to play in the experiment and explore new frontiers. Just as there is no end to this experiment of love, there is no waiting around for it to begin. We are IN the experiment RIGHT NOW.

Run Your Own Experiment No. 16:

The purpose of this experiment is to identify the deeper desires beneath our surface wants so that we can begin to build a satisfying life right now.

Experimental Procedure

1. On a piece of paper, write the header, "Why I want a husband/wife/partner/etc."

2. List all of the reasons you can come up with that you desire primary partnership, no matter how frivolous seeming.

3. Next to each, write down why you want that thing. (i.e. the things it will provide you, the problems it will solve, etc.)

4. Now, going down this list, write the deeper feeling that is looking to be satisfied.

5. Repeat step 4 as many times as is useful until you arrive at what you feel to be a base level need.

6. How can you begin to fill yourself this very moment by meeting those base needs?

Example A:

"I want someone to come home to at the end of the work day."

How would your life be different if you had someone to come home to?

"There'd be someone to hand me a glass of wine and a sympathetic ear for me to tell about the awful things my boss did that day."

How would you feel if you had this?

"I'd feel like there was someone on my side. I'd feel like I had a cheerleader. Maybe then I'd feel like I could quit this awful job. Or maybe the job wouldn't bother me as much because I'd have a whole life outside of the office."

How can you begin to provide yourself these things right now?

» Do you have other cheerleaders in your life now you could tap into?

» What steps could you take right now that would let you know you had other job options and weren't stuck?

» What's one thing you could do right now to begin building a vibrant life for yourself outside of the workplace? Sign up for a meetup in your town? Take your first guitar lesson? Invite that neighbor over for a glass of wine?

Example B:

"I want someone to take care of me financially."

How would your life be different if you had someone to provide for you financially?

"I wouldn't have to worry about paying my bills."

How would your life be different if you didn't have to worry about your bills?

"I could take the time to figure out what I really want to do with my life."

Are there any small-scale steps you could begin right now that would allow you to explore your passions? A class you could take, travel to see a friend, set up a coffee with someone who has your dream job and just begin picking their brain?

PART IV

Conclusion

PART IV

Conclusion

DEBRIEF SUMMATION

And so, we've come to the end of my observations, dear friend. May I call you that? I feel as though you know me more intimately than most now. And I must admit to you, I feel different after this journey.

The conclusions I've come to here were not the ones I anticipated at the start. I began this study, like so many of us, wanting to understand love so that I could control my romantic destiny. I both desired and feared what love could do to me, so I wanted assurance that I could decide to love the right people and keep myself safe. But at the end of all of this, I have to say I think that we control and decide very little in this field.

I no longer think I need to pin love down like an insect under glass to understand her. I no longer believe it is my job to keep myself secure amidst her chaos because I no longer believe it to be chaos. It's as though there is a much deeper, hidden, fractal-like order to the apparent chaos of love. I have more trust of her masterful planning capabilities now. So, I can more logically embrace that I do not know.

I watch my son—he's four now—and he knows the truth of this not-knowing state. It makes him the most brilliant scientist I know. His entire world is trying, testing, collecting feedback and data, processing, interpolating, trying something new. I think we must all come into this life knowing how to navigate this Grand Experiment with ease. We come in knowing that we don't know anything. But we forget. We begin to think we know ourselves, that we know the way life works. And in that knowing, we lose our spark of curiosity. We lose our ability to reinvent. We lose our playfulness in the Unknown. We trade these traits instead for fear. For self-definition and self-imposed limits. For a long list of shoulds.

I've been surprised to discover love's path in each of the relationships I've shared with you here. They have reminded me of what my son knows, that the Unknown is not something to fear or something to fix. Not knowing is not a problem. It is, in fact, an essential truth of human relationship. Now, rather than attempt to bend love's plans to my own daily insecurities (a fool's errand to be sure), I can focus on what we overthinkers do so well: preparing myself for the unknowns of love. For I believe, friend, that if you feel you are waiting around for love, you are wrong. She is waiting around for you.

I want love in my life more than ever. I want partnership and family and commitment, and with the newfound discovery that love's order has got my back, I'm now free to approach this pursuit with wholehearted curiosity. In each conclusion is the seed of a new hypothesis, and in fact, what I've learned here has already begun informing my next set of experiments, ones I'll track in the form of a podcast I call *Curious Love*. Step by step, awkward conversation by awkward conversation, I am going to methodically seek out the Unknown with open arms and earnest interest in preparing myself to become someone's beloved. It bolsters me to think of you as a part of my support team, lending me your bravery as a fellow explorer, ready to receive my reports from uncharted territory and uncover new truths alongside me. I will not fail you.

No matter where you are in your own experiments, now is the perfect time to get your ducks in a row so you can say "yes!" to love whenever and however she arrives. You've already begun just by being in this inquiry. You already know that there is nothing that another human being can give you that you cannot begin to cultivate in yourself this moment. You've followed the threads of your hopes for relationship, and you've begun to investigate the deep yearnings they point to so that you can step up for yourself and begin meeting them right now. You've practiced calling up the well-spring of love within, and you know that if you are waiting for someone to love you, you can start loving yourself immediately. Feel loving right now. Feel loved right now. *Right Now.*

This is fantastic news! You are an adult, present now, accepting of what is right now, responsible for your own actions, your own life, your own joy, and you are able to begin filling the cup of yourself now. And here's the secret bonus. In this preparation, you become more fit for love, you become a better mate, and you will begin to recognize others who are equally responsible, whole, and actively cultivating themselves for a joyful, thriving relationship.

It's time, now. Will you go into the field of your own life, ready to jump into the experiment and discover who you are in love? Will you report back with your own experiences and data? Will you contribute a conclusion to the Love Lab and inspire another collaborator's next great experiment at experimentsinlove.com? Or perhaps you'll drop us a line just to let us know you're out there. I'll be here waiting for you, cheering you on, and supporting your endeavors however I can.

Go on, now. The playground of the unknown awaits you. I hope to see you out there.

Talk Soon,
Your Fellow Scientist, Subject, and Seeker
(and Proud Overthinker)

Kristen Ruth Smith

ADDITIONAL
EXPERIMENTAL NOTES

Amanda; Chapter 4; Experiment 110.42.2
Nine months after she returned my things, Amanda left the insurance company. I never saw her or spoke to her in person again. Some experiments never manage to bear satisfying results.

Jonah; Chapters 6, 7, 9; Experiments 140.22.8, 140.40.3, 140.70.1
Jonah and I have found a rhythm that successfully lets our son know he's loved by lots and lots of people on both sides of his family tree.

Naomi; Chapters 10–12; Experiments 130.10.04, 151.11.5, 151.22.0
Naomi and I decided that our connection was valuable enough to find a new way to be in friendship with one another. Each day continues to be a new opportunity for experiment.

Curious about what happens next?

Check out *Curious Love,* the eight-episode podcast serial that picks up where this story leaves off.

Join Kristen for the next phase of her earnest and intimate quest to solve the mystery of partnership as she risks embarrassing conversations and awkward confrontations with experts, friends, and family alike.

Learn more at *www.curious-love.com.*